96

Understanding

# Of Mice
# and Men

New and future titles in the Understanding Great Literature series include:

Understanding *The Catcher in the Rye*
Understanding *Flowers for Algernon*
Understanding *The Great Gatsby*
Understanding *I Am the Cheese*
Understanding *Macbeth*
Understanding *The Outsiders*
Understanding *Romeo and Juliet*
Understanding *The Yearling*

Understanding

# Of Mice and Men

UNDERSTANDING GREAT LITERATURE

**Bradley Steffens**

Lucent Books
10911 Technology Place
San Diego, CA 92127

# FOREWORD

"Except for a living man, there is nothing more wonderful than a book!" wrote the widely respected nineteenth-century teacher and writer Charles Kingsley. A book, he continued, "is a message to us from human souls we never saw. And yet these [books] arouse us, terrify us, teach us, comfort us, open our hearts to us as brothers." There are many different kinds of books, of course; and Kingsley was referring mainly to those containing literature—novels, plays, short stories, poems, and so on. In particular, he had in mind those works of literature that were and remain widely popular with readers of all ages and from many walks of life.

Such popularity might be based on one or several factors. On the one hand, a book might be read and studied by people in generation after generation because it is a literary classic, with characters and themes of universal relevance and appeal. Homer's epic poems, the *Iliad* and the *Odyssey*, Chaucer's *Canterbury Tales*, Shakespeare's *Hamlet* and *Romeo and Juliet*, and Dickens's *A Christmas Carol* fall into this category. Some popular books, on the other hand, are more controversial. Mark Twain's *Huckleberry Finn* and J. D. Salinger's *The Catcher in the Rye*, for instance, have their legions of devoted fans who see them as great literature; while others view them as less than worthy because of their racial depictions, profanity, or other factors.

Still another category of popular literature includes realistic modern fiction, including novels such as Robert Cormier's *I Am the Cheese* and S. E. Hinton's *The Outsiders*. Their keen social insights and sharp character portrayals have consistently reached out to and captured the imaginations of many teen-agers and young adults; and for this reason they are often assigned and studied in schools.

These and other similar works have become the "old stan-dards" of the literary scene. They are the ones that people most often read, discuss, and study; and each has, by virtue of its con-tent, critical success, or just plain longevity, earned the right to be the subject of a book examining its content. (Some, of course, like the *Iliad* and *Hamlet*, have been the subjects of numerous books already; but their literary stature is so lofty that there can never be too many books about them!) For mil-lions of readers and students in one generation after another, each of these works becomes, in a sense, an adventure in appre-ciation, enjoyment, and learning.

The main purpose of Lucent's Understanding Great Literature series is to aid the reader in that ongoing literary adventure. Each volume in the series focuses on a single liter-ary work that a majority of critics and teachers view as a classic and/or that is widely studied and discussed in schools. A typi-cal volume first tells why the work in question is important. Then follow detailed overviews of the author's life, the work's historical background, its plot, its characters, and its themes. Numerous quotes from the work, as well as by critics and other experts, are interspersed throughout and carefully document-ed with footnotes for those who wish to pursue further research. Also included is a list of ideas for essays and other stu-dent projects relating to the work, an appendix of literary criti-cisms and analyses by noted scholars, and a comprehensive annotated bibliography.

The great nineteenth-century American poet Henry David Thoreau once quipped: "Read the best books first, or you may not have a chance to read them at all." For those who are read-ing or about to read the "best books" in the literary canon, the comprehensive, thorough, and thoughtful volumes of the Understanding Great Literature series are indispensable guides and sources of enrichment.

# Theater of the Mind

When *Of Mice and Men* was published in 1937, many people were surprised at the narrow scope of the book and the simplicity of its plot. It was quite unlike Steinbeck's earlier novels, *Cup of Gold* and *In Dubious Battle*. Although some critics praised the book for its realism and compassion, others found it to be so simple as to be mechanical. "Lennie, you see, cannot help shaking small helpless creatures until their necks are broken, just as George cannot relinquish his dream, and just as Curley cannot ever stop being a beast of jealousy," wrote critic Mark Van Doren shortly after the book appeared. "They are wound up to act that way, and the best they can do is run down; which is what happens when Mr. Steinbeck comes to his last mechanical page."[1]

At least part of the criticism aimed at the book arose from its failure to live up to traditional expectations of what a novel is and what it can be. *Of Mice and Men* lacks the scope and complexity of titanic works such as *The Brothers Karamazov*, *Moby-Dick*, or *Ulysses*. Its plot is simpler and its view of the world even narrower than that of such short novels as *The Great Gatsby*. In addition, Steinbeck did not make use of such novelistic techniques as having action take place in several places at once, having the narrator comment in depth on the events in the story, revealing the internal thoughts of the characters, and so forth. In fact, *Of Mice and Men* was not intended to be a novel at all but a type of play, one performed not on a stage but in the theater of the mind. "The work I am doing now is neither a novel nor a play but a kind of playable novel," Steinbeck wrote to his literary agents in 1936. "It wouldn't be like other plays since it does not follow the formal acts but uses chapters for curtains."[2]

Even readers who know nothing about Steinbeck's stated intentions will instantly recognize the playlike qualities of the book. Each chapter opens with a long description of a physical place, much like a playwright's description of a set. All of the chapter's action takes place in that scene or else nearby. Events take place in real time; once the characters enter the scene, the narrator rarely interrupts the flow of action to comment on their behavior or to add any discourse of his own. Everything about the characters' past and present lives is revealed through their speech and actions, just as in a play.

Although the plots of many plays are extremely complex, some of the most successful plays are very simple. The medieval morality play *Everyman,* for example, creates a full dramatic experience with a plot that critic Otto Reinhart describes as "uncomplicated to the point of nonexistence."[3] The same is true of the more modern plays such as Anton Chekhov's *Three Sisters* and Samuel Beckett's *Waiting for Godot.* These works achieve meaning, beauty, and suspense through a variety of techniques, such as the repetition of key words and images. Steinbeck borrowed from this dramatic tradition, relying on the speech of his characters to intrigue, enchant, and illuminate the reader.

Shortly after the book was published, Steinbeck revised *Of Mice and Men* for the stage, keeping roughly 85 percent of the dialogue as originally written. The play was hailed as a success, edging out Thornton Wilder's *Our Town* to win the

*Shown is a scene from* Waiting for Godot. *It has a simplistic plot much like* Of Mice and Men.

Drama Critics Circle Award for best play in 1937. The drama was adapted as a motion picture in 1939 and in 1992, as a television drama in 1968 and 1981, and as an opera in 1970. Whether on the stage, the screen, or in the theater of the mind, *Of Mice and Men* achieves immortality by presenting a simple, brief tableau of two men sharing a common dream and an uncommon bond.

# CHAPTER ONE

# The Life of John Steinbeck

S tretching from the Gabilan Mountains in the east to the Santa Lucia Range in the west, the fertile Salinas Valley of west-central California was home to John Ernst Steinbeck; his wife, Olive Hamilton Steinbeck; their daughters, Esther, Elizabeth, and Mary; and their son, also named John. It also was the birthplace of dozens of imaginary characters that the younger John Steinbeck would create over his lifetime—lifelike and memorable characters who eventually would earn him the Nobel Prize for literature.

Located on the Salinas River, the town of Salinas was a center of agricultural commerce. Not surprisingly, John Ernst Steinbeck tried his hand in the agriculture business, working in a flour mill and later operating a feed-and-grain store. The store eventually failed, so he turned to accounting to support his family. Although far from wealthy, John Ernst and Olive Steinbeck lived in a large house at 130 Central Avenue, where the younger John Ernst was born on February 27, 1902.

Reading was a popular pastime in the Steinbeck home. The family read aloud for entertainment, and Olive Steinbeck took care to introduce her children to literature at an early age. She read the Bible to John when he was just three years old. By the time he was four, she was reading him such classic stories as *Robin Hood* and *Treasure Island*.

## A Magical Experience

Although it was John's mother who fostered his early interest in books and literature, it was his aunt who gave him the book that would change his life. For John's ninth birthday his aunt presented him with an abridged version of Sir Thomas Malory's account of the legendary King Arthur and his knights of the Round Table, *Le Morte D'Arthur.* Later, Steinbeck described how the book came to hold a special place in his life:

> I stared at the black print with hatred, and then gradually the pages opened and let me in. The magic happened. The Bible and Shakespeare and *Pilgrim's Progress* belonged to everyone. But this was mine—secretly mine. . . . I loved the old spellings of the words—and words no longer used. Perhaps a passionate love for the English language opened to me from this one book.[4]

John shared the wonders of this secret book with his younger sister Mary, and the two children often acted out the adventures of King Arthur and his knights of the Round Table. Steinbeck's love of the King Arthur legend lasted a lifetime and later surfaced in his own fiction.

For his twelfth birthday, John's parents surprised him with a pony, which John kept at a stable in town. In addition to his regular household chores, John fed, curried, and brushed the pony, named Jill, and kept her stall clean. Many years later John drew on his experiences with Jill when he wrote one of his most beloved short novels, *The Red Pony.*

When he was thirteen, John enrolled in Salinas High School, a two-story brick building with an enrollment of

*John Steinbeck's boyhood home in Salinas, California.*

about two hundred students. At the time, high school began in eighth grade and lasted five years. An average student in most subjects, Steinbeck excelled in English. He began to write for the school newspaper, *El Gabilan,* and began to think seriously of becoming a writer. "You know, I write the purest English of anyone in the world,"[5] he once remarked to a classmate. A contribution he made to his high school yearbook shows his emerging talent and wit:

> The English room, which is just down the hall from the office, is the sanctuary of Shakespeare, the temple of Milton and Byron, and the terror of Freshmen. English is a kind of high brow idea of the American language. A hard job is made of nothing at all and nothing at all is made of a hard job. It is in this room and this room alone that the English language is spoken.[6]

## Valuable Lessons

Steinbeck graduated from high school in 1919 and enrolled in Stanford University in the fall. He attended classes on and off for six years but never earned a degree. Stanford proved important to Steinbeck's growth as a writer, however, for there he met Edith Ronald Mirrielees, a dedicated and demanding English professor who taught a class titled "Short Story Writing." Mirrielees recognized Steinbeck's talent but urged him to simplify his writing by using the fewest possible

*Steinbeck, photographed while a student at Stanford University.*

words to express an idea. It was a difficult lesson for the self-professed lover of words, but Steinbeck slowly began to appreciate the value of the spare writing style that would eventually become his personal hallmark. "She does one thing for you," Steinbeck wrote to a friend about Mirrielees. "She makes you get over what you want to say. Her only vicious criticism is directed toward turgidity, and that is a good thing."[7]

While at Stanford, Steinbeck managed to publish two stories in the *Stanford Spectator.* One was a satire about college life titled "Adventures in Arcademy: A Journey into the Ridiculous." The other, "Fingers of Cloud: A Satire on College Protervity," tells the story of a mentally impaired young woman who marries a migrant worker. In both stories Steinbeck mixed elements of realism, fantasy, and allegory, just as he would in his later fiction. He also published three poems in the Stanford literary magazine.

The classroom was not the only place that Steinbeck received his education as a writer. During the summers that he attended high school and college, Steinbeck worked on various ranches and farms in the Salinas Valley, including the Spreckels Sugar Company's sugar-beet farm and processing plant. These stints of manual labor taught Steinbeck valuable lessons about life and gave him scenes and events that he would later use in his stories. "I worked in the same country that [*Of Mice and Men*] is laid in," Steinbeck later told reporters after the novel was published. "The characters are composites to a certain extent. Lennie was a real person. He's in an insane asylum in California right now. I worked alongside him for many weeks. He didn't kill a girl. He killed a ranch foreman. Got sore because the boss had fired his pal and stuck a pitchfork right through his stomach."[8]

## Journey to New York
Steinbeck left Stanford in 1925, saved up some money, and took a job as a caretaker at a resort in Lake Tahoe in the Sierra

Nevada mountains. In his free time, Steinbeck wrote. He polished his old short stories and began new ones. He also worked on a novel he had started in college about the English buccaneer Sir Henry Morgan. When the summer came to an end, Steinbeck left Lake Tahoe. In November, he took a job on a freight ship bound for New York City, where he planned to pursue his writing career in earnest. The young man from the sparsely populated valleys of California was not prepared for life in America's largest city. "It horrified me," Steinbeck later recalled. "There was something monstrous about it— the tall buildings looming to the sky and the lights shining through the falling snow. I crept ashore—frightened and cold with a touch of panic in my stomach."[9]

Steinbeck supported himself by working on the construction of the old Madison Square Garden building in Manhattan. The sturdy young man wheeled 150-pound barrowfuls of cement around the construction site so ably that when he left the job, his foreman told him, "I'm sorry to lose you, my boy. You've got the makings of a darn good day laborer."[10]

With the help of his uncle, Joe Hamilton, Steinbeck was able to secure a job as a reporter with a Hearst newspaper, the *New York American*. Although he was supporting himself with his writing, Steinbeck lacked the type of discipline needed to be a successful reporter. He chafed under the pressure of tight deadlines, and he sometimes became emotionally involved with the people and stories he covered, losing the required professional distance. Nevertheless, the young writer continued to learn more about his craft. "I worked for the *American* and was assigned to the Federal Court in the old Park Row post office where I did some lousy reporting," Steinbeck later recalled. "I did, however, perfect a certain literary versatility."[11]

In his spare time, Steinbeck continued to work on his short stories and his often-revised novel. Through a friend, Steinbeck met Guy Holt, an editor with Robert M. McBride

*New York City offered Steinbeck a new venue for developing his writing career.*

and Company. Steinbeck showed Holt some of his short stories. The editor liked Steinbeck's work and encouraged the young writer to complete a few more stories and then submit a collection for publication. By the time Steinbeck did so, however, Holt had left McBride. Holt's replacement rejected Steinbeck's manuscript. Dejected, Steinbeck decided to leave New York. He later recalled, "Whatever it required to get ahead, I didn't have."[12]

## Professional Publication

Steinbeck returned to California the same way he had gone to New York—by working on a freighter. After a brief reunion with his family, Steinbeck returned to Lake Tahoe, where he got a job as a caretaker at a large estate owned by Alice Brigham. In the isolated serenity of the mountain town, Steinbeck continued to work on his novel about Sir Henry Morgan. As he toiled over the manuscript, Steinbeck received news of his first professional publication. A magazine called the *Smoker's Companion* agreed to publish one of his short stories, "The Gifts of Iban," in its March 1927 issue. Encouraged by this news, Steinbeck continued to work on the novel, which he called *Cup of Gold*. He completed the book in February 1928 and mailed the manuscript to Ted Miller, a for-

*A worker tends to a fish pool at a hatchery. Steinbeck met his future wife while working at a fish hatchery.*

mer Stanford classmate who lived in New York. Miller promised Steinbeck that he would act as his literary agent, showing his work to various publishers.

While in Lake Tahoe, Steinbeck took a job at a fish hatchery. One day, he spotted an attractive young woman who was taking a tour of the facility. Steinbeck introduced himself to the pretty tourist, whose name was Carol Henning, and the two agreed to see each other later. Steinbeck and Henning dated for several days in Lake Tahoe before Henning returned to her home in San Francisco. Determined to continue seeing Henning, Steinbeck quit his job at the hatchery and moved to San Francisco in the fall of 1928.

Steinbeck got a job in a warehouse, but the physical labor left him too tired to write very much. Steinbeck's father became concerned that his son was not pursuing his budding writing career, so he offered to let him live rent-free in the family cottage in Pacific Grove and to provide him twenty-five dollars a month for expenses. Steinbeck accepted the offer. He quit the warehouse job and moved to Pacific Grove, where he worked on his writing and saw Henning on weekends.

Late in 1928 Steinbeck received the news he had been waiting for ever since he had shipped *Cup of Gold* off to New York. True to his word, Ted Miller had offered the manuscript to several publishing houses, including the one that had rejected Steinbeck's short story collection, Robert M. McBride and Company. The editors at McBride were impressed with *Cup of Gold* and awarded Steinbeck a contract to publish the book. Though not a critical or financial success, *Cup of Gold* confirmed the twenty-six-year-old writer's belief in himself.

## Marriage

After the publication of *Cup of Gold* in 1929, Steinbeck and Henning announced their engagement. In December they set off for Los Angeles, arriving in January 1930. On January 14

Steinbeck and Henning got married in a civil ceremony in Glendale, California. They rented a house in the town of Eagle Rock. A secretary by profession, Carol looked for work while John continued writing stories. Employment was scarce, however, because the New York Stock Exchange had crashed in October 1929, and by 1930 the entire country had plunged into the financial crisis known as the Great Depression. Because of this downturn, more than twenty-six thousand businesses failed in 1930 alone. Unemployment rose from 3 percent before the crash to 9 percent in early 1930. Within two years, 25 percent of the workforce would be unemployed. Unable to collect on their investments, thousands of banks simply closed their doors, causing millions of Americans to lose their savings. Steinbeck remained philosophical about the hard times. "The Depression was no financial shock to me," he later recalled. "I didn't have money to lose, but in common with millions I did dislike hunger and cold."[13]

With the small advance from *Cup of Gold* dwindling and Carol unable to find work, the Steinbecks retreated to the family cottage in Pacific Grove. Thanks to the generosity of John's father, the young couple was able to live in the tiny three-room cottage without paying rent. Along the nearby beach, John collected driftwood to burn for heat. He also turned to the sea for food. "People in inland cities or in the closed and shuttered industrial cemeteries had greater problems than I," he later recalled. "Given the sea a man must be very stupid to starve. The great reservoir of food is always available. I took a large part of my protein food from the sea."[14]

## An Important Friendship

During this time, Steinbeck met Edward F. Ricketts, a marine biologist whose ideas about nature fascinated the young novelist and began to influence his view of life and his approach to fiction. Ricketts observed and recorded marine life as objectively as possible. Watching as organisms competed rigorously for survival in a harsh and hostile world, Ricketts developed a belief that nature was nonteleological—that is, guided by no philosophical principles and serving no purpose other than the sustenance of life. He looked at things as they are, rather than how they should be. Steinbeck began to apply these principles to his observations of human beings. He discarded romantic notions about mankind occupying a special place in nature or being guided toward any special ends. He decided that as a writer he would not pass judgment on human behavior any more than he would on the behavior of a shark, a starfish, or an anemone. Slowly he purged his writing of philosophical speculation, focusing instead on characters, events, and consequences.

In addition to being energized by his friendship with Ricketts, Steinbeck was helped in his writing by Carol, an accomplished secretary who volunteered to type his manuscripts. With the time to write, new ideas to ponder, and his wife's assistance, Steinbeck produced a great deal of new work. He worked on a novel called *Dissonant Harmony* and a detective story, *Murder at Full Moon*. He wrote a collection of ten short stories about a family named Munroe and worked on a novel about families from New England that had settled in the Salinas Valley. He never completed *Dissonant Harmony,* and *Murder at Full Moon* was never published. However, the ten short stories were published by McBride in 1932 under the title *Pastures of Heaven.* The novel *To a God Unknown,* set in the Salinas Valley, was published in 1933. Neither book sold well. Although Steinbeck had published three books, he could not quite consider his career a success.

## Achievement and Loss

Not long after the publication of *To a God Unknown,* Olive Steinbeck suffered a stroke, and John and Carol traveled to Salinas to help John's father care for her. Although the

*Spencer Tracy (left) and Hedy Lamarr starred in the 1942 production of*
Tortilla Flat, *a film based on Steinbeck's novel.*

circumstances of the visit were emotionally difficult, Steinbeck's return to his boyhood home sparked several ideas for
new stories. Conversations with his father led Steinbeck to con-
ceive a group of short stories that would be published under
the title *The Red Pony.* He also envisioned writing a story about
a group of poor Mexicans known as *paisanos.* As he helped care
for his mother, Steinbeck received word that two of his stories
were to appear in the *North American Review.* The same journal published a third Steinbeck short story, "The Murder," the
next year. In addition to money, the sale of these stories began
to bring the young writer a bit of recognition. "The Murder"
won the O. Henry Award for the best short story of 1934.

Despite the loss of his mother, who died in 1934, Steinbeck completed his novel about the *paisanos,* which he titled
*Tortilla Flat,* and submitted it to five different publishers, each

of whom turned him down. In January 1935 the sixth publisher Steinbeck contacted, Pascal Covici, snapped up the manuscript. The lighthearted story of the *paisanos,* whose adventures are like those of King Arthur's knights, was an immediate success. Not only did the book become a bestseller, but a motion picture company also purchased the rights to the book for four thousand dollars—a huge sum of money at the time.

Having achieved a measure of critical, popular, and financial success, Steinbeck began work on a novel about the struggles of a labor movement in the agricultural area where Steinbeck himself had worked. Published in 1936, *In Dubious Battle* sold well and added to Steinbeck's growing reputation. These achievements were tempered, however, by the death of Steinbeck's father in 1936.

## A New Form

With the money from book royalties and movie rights, John and Carol Steinbeck decided to build a home in Los Gatos, California. As Carol oversaw the construction of the house, John worked on a new book. Again Steinbeck turned to his beloved Salinas Valley as a setting for the story, but this time he decided to experiment with a different form of writing. "I'm going into training to write for the theatre, which seems to be waking up," he wrote to a friend at the time. "I have some ideas for a new dramatic form which I'm experimenting with."[15] The new form Steinbeck had in mind was a hybrid between a novel and a play. "*Of Mice and Men* was an attempt to write a novel in three acts to be played from the lines," Steinbeck later explained. "This book had some success, but as usual found its enemies. With rewriting, however, it did become a play and had some success."[16]

Published in February 1937, *Of Mice and Men* was an instant hit, selling a thousand copies a day in its first few weeks. Steinbeck collaborated with playwright George S. Kaufman to create a stage version in November of that year. The play garnered excellent reviews and won the Drama Critics Circle Award. Two years later, the script was adapted for motion pictures by Eugene Solow. Directed by Lewis Milestone and starring Lon Chaney Jr. and Burgess Meredith, the movie made John Steinbeck a household name.

Following the success of *Of Mice and Men,* Steinbeck settled in to write a novel about migrant workers. The result of these efforts was *The Grapes of Wrath,* the epic story of Oklahoma farmers who migrate from the Dust Bowl to California. Published in 1939, the book received widespread critical acclaim and proved to be one of the most popular books of the year, selling more than four hundred thousand copies. Many critics consider *The Grapes of Wrath* to be Steinbeck's masterpiece. It received the Pulitzer Prize for fiction in 1940. Sixty

*A young Henry Fonda (center) and fellow actors portray Oklahoma farmers in a film adaptation of* The Grapes of Wrath.

years after it was published, a board of literary scholars working for Modern Library ranked *The Grapes of Wrath* tenth on its list of the one hundred best novels of the twentieth century. A film version of the story was released in 1940, bringing the story to millions more. Directed by John Ford and starring Henry Fonda, the movie was ranked twenty-first on the American Film Institute's list of the one hundred greatest American films.

## World War II

In 1940 Steinbeck accompanied Edward Ricketts on a specimen-gathering trip to the Gulf of Mexico. Steinbeck and Ricketts collaborated on an account of this trip that was published in 1941 as *Sea of Cortez*. In December of that year, Japanese forces attacked the U.S. naval base at Pearl Harbor and the United States entered World War II. Like millions of other Americans, Steinbeck turned his attention to the war. He wrote a story about a town occupied by German troops titled *The Moon Is Down*. He also wrote *Bombs Away: The Story of a Bomber Team*. In 1943 a film version of *The Moon Is Down* was released.

Although Steinbeck's career was going well, his personal life was not. Carol had become attracted to one of his friends, the anthropologist Joseph Campbell, which had caused a rift in the marriage. The two separated, and Steinbeck met and fell in love with a vivacious radio singer named Gwendolyn Conger. As soon as his divorce from Carol became official, Steinbeck married Conger on March 29, 1943. Shortly after the wedding, Steinbeck received permission to travel to Europe as a war correspondent. He filed insightful and sometimes humorous dispatches that mainly described life behind the fighting lines. Returning to the United States, Steinbeck wrote the lighthearted novel *Cannery Row*, which he called "a kind of nostalgia thing, written for a group of soldiers who had said to me, 'Write something funny that isn't about the war.'"[17] Set on the waterfront of Monterey, California, the story features a character named Doc who is a fictionalized version of Ricketts. Continuing his association with Hollywood, Steinbeck also collaborated with director Alfred Hitchcock on the screenplay for the movie *Lifeboat.*

## Family Man

John and Gwendolyn lived in Monterey for a year, then moved to New York City. In 1944 Gwendolyn gave birth to their first son, Thom. Two years later, the couple celebrated the birth of a second son, John. Meanwhile, Steinbeck was hard at work on two more books. In 1947 he published *The Pearl,* the story of a poor fisherman whose life is changed when he finds an enormous pearl, and *The Wayward Bus,* a story about a busload of tourists who act out a kind of morality play. In what had become a Steinbeck tradition, both books would eventually find their way onto the movie screen.

In 1948 Steinbeck received the shocking news that Ricketts had been seriously injured in a car accident. Steinbeck rushed from New York to Monterey to be at his friend's side. When Ricketts died a few days later, Steinbeck was heartbroken. "There died the greatest man I have known and the best teacher. It is going to take a long time to reorganize my thinking and my planning without him."[18] Shortly after Ricketts's death, John and Gwendolyn divorced.

## A Happy Union

In 1950 Steinbeck married Elaine Scott, the former wife of the movie actor Zachary Scott. Steinbeck's third marriage was a happy one, and the world-famous novelist began to write with renewed vigor. He produced a second play-novella, *Burning Bright.* Like *Of Mice and Men, Burning Bright* was produced as a stage play. He also wrote the screenplay for the motion picture *Viva Zapata!* In 1952 Steinbeck published *East of Eden,* the book he believed to be his best.

*John Steinbeck poses with his third wife, Elaine Scott.*

Though the critics were not pleased with the contemporary retelling of the biblical story of Cain and Abel, *East of Eden* became a best-seller and, like other Steinbeck successes, was adapted for motion pictures.

Following the publication of *East of Eden,* the Steinbecks took an extended trip to Europe, visiting Italy, France, and the birthplace of John's grandparents in Ireland. When the couple returned to the United States in 1955, they purchased a home in Sag Harbor, Long Island, close to the ocean. Although the house needed renovation, Steinbeck loved it, nicknaming it Cannery Row East. "What John liked was the fact that the house had possibilities," Elaine Steinbeck later recalled. "It had to be imagined. The main thing about it was really the sea. John had been longing to live near the water."[19]

During the 1950s Steinbeck devoted himself to translating Malory's *Le Morte D'Arthur*. The nearly completed but unfinished work, known as *The Acts of King Arthur and His Noble Knights*, was not published until after his death. Steinbeck also wrote a sequel to the critically panned *Cannery Row*. The new book, *Sweet Thursday*, was published in 1954. The critics were no more impressed with the sequel than they were with the original. In 1957 Steinbeck published another book that received harsh reviews, a fable titled *The Short Reign of Pippin IV, a Fabrication*.

In 1958 Steinbeck published a collection of his World War II dispatches under the title *Once There Was a War*. Two years later Steinbeck produced his last novel, *The Winter of Our Discontent*. While the book was being prepared for publication, Steinbeck took a cross-country camping trip with Elaine's poodle, Charley. This journey formed the basis for his 1962 book *Travels with Charley in Search of America*.

## Recognition

As the 1960s dawned, Steinbeck began to receive recognition for his lifetime of work. Newly elected president John F. Kennedy invited Steinbeck to his 1961 inauguration. Steinbeck's greatest honor came a year later, when he was awarded the Nobel Prize for literature. His Nobel acceptance address was a stirring tribute to the values he championed as a writer —compassion, honesty, courage, and hope:

> The writer is delegated to declare and to celebrate man's proven capacity for greatness of heart and spirit—for gallantry in defeat, for courage, compassion and love. In the endless war against weakness and despair, these are the bright rally flags of hope and of emulation. I hold that a writer who does not passionately believe in the perfectibility of man has no dedication nor any membership in literature.[20]

After President Kennedy's assassination in 1963, Steinbeck became friends with his successor, Lyndon Johnson. Johnson frequently invited Steinbeck to the White House throughout his presidency. In 1964 Johnson awarded Steinbeck the U.S. Medal of Freedom. That same year, Steinbeck was named a trustee of the John F. Kennedy Memorial Library. In 1966 the famous author was elected to the National Arts Council.

*In 1962, Steinbeck (right) received the Nobel Prize for Literature from Sweden's King Gustav Adolph.*

In 1965 Steinbeck traveled to Vietnam to report on the war for *Newsday,* a Long Island newspaper. He returned to the United States in failing health. In late 1967 he had spinal fusion surgery to relieve pain in his back. The following year he suffered a stroke and a series of heart attacks. On December 20, 1968, Steinbeck died in New York City at the age of sixty-six. In accordance with his final wishes, Elaine Steinbeck returned her husband's cremated remains to the valley between the Santa Lucia and Gabilan Mountains, where his life and literature had begun.

CHAPTER TWO

# The Impact of the Novel

John Steinbeck sent *Of Mice and Men* to his agents without a strong feeling about its success as a work of art. He considered it a sketchbook and was not surprised when his agents found the book to be limited in scope. Steinbeck took complete responsibility for the book's shortcomings. "I'm sorry that you do not find the new book as large in subject as it should be," he wrote. "I probably did not make my subjects and symbols clear."[21]

Steinbeck's agents probably had hoped that their young talent would reproduce the success of his previous novel, *In Dubious Battle*. Perhaps they expected him to attempt something even broader in scope. Given the tendency of publishers to charge less money for a thin book than for a thick one, it is possible that the agents' disappointment with *Of Mice and Men* was entirely mercenary.

## Best-seller

Steinbeck's publisher, Pascal Covici, did not share the agents' misgivings. He considered the book a gem and accepted it with enthusiasm. Published in February 1937, *Of Mice and Men* was the Book-of-the-Month Club offering for that March. Exposure to the club members made *Of Mice and*

Of Mice and Men *was published in 1937 and became a best-selling novel.*

*Men* an instant best-seller. By the end of the year, more than one hundred thousand copies of the book had been sold.

Reviews of the book were mixed. Henry Seidel Canby praised the book in the *Saturday Review* for its "good storytelling," and Lewis Gannet lauded it for its "compassion."[22] Writing for the *Nation* in 1937, however, critic Mark Van Doren panned the book for its lack of realistic characters and motivations. "Mr. Steinbeck, I take it, has not been interested in reality of any kind," Van Doren wrote. "All but one of the persons in Mr. Steinbeck's extremely brief novel are subhuman," Van Doren declared. He wrote that the one character who was not subhuman, Slim, is "as hopelessly above the human range as Lennie or Candy or Curley's painted wife is below it. All is extreme here; everybody is a doll."[23]

## Successful Staging

Having originally conceived *Of Mice and Men* as a drama, Steinbeck began to revise his story for the stage shortly after its publication. He collaborated with successful playwright and director George S. Kaufman to produce a script, and the play opened at the Music Box Theater in New York in November 1937. The drama received rave reviews. Critic John Mason Brown found the play to be "the most poignant statement of human loneliness our contemporary theatre has produced."[24] Brooks Atkinson of the *New York Times* praised Steinbeck and Kaufman for achieving "lyric perfection" out of "rude materials."[25]

Writing for the *English Journal,* author and critic Burton Rascoe deemed the play "an aesthetic miracle." After noting how audiences had a tendency to laugh at the opening scenes, as if the play were a comedy, Rascoe wrote that by the end of the evening "the light, superficially cynical mood of the less sensitive members of the audience has changed, and pity and wonder has taken possession of them. This is the miracle I referred to in the opening sentences of this discourse."[26]

Rascoe compared the play to a Greek tragedy in which the outcome of the plot is foreseeable long before it occurs but which enthralls the audience with the art of its particulars. "The impatient, plot-minded reader doesn't have to turn to the back of the book to see how it comes out," wrote Rascoe. "Steinbeck tells you, in effect, in the first five pages just about how it is 'going to come out'. And that is his terrific moral."[27]

Fifteen of the sixteen of the voting members of the Drama Critics Circle Awards praised the play when it opened, so it was no surprise that the group honored *Of Mice and Men* as the best play of 1937. The citation that accompanied the award described the virtues that have made both the play and the novel a modern classic:

> For its direct force and perception in handling a theme genuinely rooted in American life; for its bite into the strict quality of its material; for its refusal to make this study of tragic loneliness and frustration either cheap or sensational, and finally for its simple, intense and steadily rising effect on the stage.[28]

Two years after the play debuted, Lewis Milestone brought Steinbeck's story to the motion-picture screen "miraculously intact in mood and spirit,"[29] according to *Theatre Arts* magazine. With a screenplay by Eugene Solow, the movie featured Lon Chaney Jr. as Lennie and Burgess Meredith as George. The acclaimed American composer Aaron Copland wrote the score.

*Lon Chaney Jr. (left) starred as Lennie and Burgess Meredith (right) starred as George in the 1939 film version* Of Mice and Men.

## Controversial Language

From the outset, *Of Mice and Men* was condemned for the vulgar language uttered by its characters. A reviewer for the *Catholic World* wrote, "The first few pages so nauseated me that I couldn't bear to keep it in my room over night."[30] "The bunk house talk is terrific," Mark Van Doren sarcastically observed in his review of the book for the *Nation*. "God damn, Jesus Christ, what the hell, you crazy bastard, I gotta gut ache and things like that. The dialect never varies."[31] The *New York Times* reported that members of the clergy in Fort Mc-Clellan, Alabama, condemned the motion-picture version as "morbid and degenerate,"[32] causing a showing of the movie to be canceled.

Misgivings about the language and themes of the book continue to the present time. The American Library Association reports that *Of Mice and Men* ranks sixth among the top one hundred books most frequently requested to be removed from library shelves, far ahead of such works as J.D. Salinger's *Catcher in the Rye* and Madonna's *Sex*. The September 1990 issue of *Writer's Digest* stated that *Of Mice and Men* was among the top three books most often removed from library and school bookshelves.

Steinbeck did not intend to shock his audience with the language of his characters, only to accurately reproduce the speech of the types of people portrayed in his books. "To the men I write about profanity is adornment and ornament and is never vulgar," Steinbeck wrote in a 1939 letter, "and I try to write so."[33] By writing such gritty and convincing dialogue, Steinbeck broke new ground for writers of his generation and those to follow.

His tale of two men and their shared dream continues to enchant and inspire readers of all ages.

# CHAPTER THREE

# The Plot

I n keeping with his idea of writing a type of drama that used "chapters for curtains,"[34] Steinbeck did not give titles to the chapters of *Of Mice and Men* nor did he number them. Each new section of the book begins halfway down the printed page, the blank paper stretching like a white curtain above the text. By omitting chapter titles, Steinbeck refrains from commenting on the events that follow, leaving the reader to experience them as if watching a play.

## Beside the Pool

The first chapter opens with a detailed description of an area around a narrow pool. Into this idyllic setting enter two men: one small with sharply defined features followed by one who is the opposite—large with a shapeless face. Dressed in the denim clothes typically worn by ranch workers, the two men stop beside the pool. As the smaller man watches, the larger man flings himself onto the ground, puts his face in the water, and drinks the surface like an animal. The smaller man calls the larger man by his name, Lennie, and warns him not to drink so much. Instead of heeding his companion's advice, Lennie dips his head underwater and takes a last huge gulp. Satisfied, the large man invites his friend, George, to take a drink. George nervously dips his hand into the water and scoops out small sips. While admitting that the water tastes good, George notes that the water is not moving and cautions Lennie against drinking standing water. Though few words have been spoken, it is clear that although the two men are roughly the same age, George watches out for and guides Lennie much as a parent does a child. Lennie does not resist George's guidance but more or less conforms to it, confirming the adult/child relationship.

As the two men sit on the bank of the pool, Lennie asks where they are going. George reminds Lennie that he has already told him their plans and that Lennie must have forgotten. Frustrated, George calls Lennie "crazy." Lennie apologizes for forgetting, and George softens toward his companion. "O.K. I'll tell ya again. I ain't got nothing to do. Might jus' as well spen' all my time tellin' you things and then you forget 'em, and I tell you again."[35] With this exchange, the reason for George and Lennie's adult/child relationship becomes clear: Lennie is mentally incapable of remembering things or taking care of himself.

*The adult/child relationship between George and Lennie is revealed in the opening scene of both the novel and the film.*

When Lennie continually puts one of his hands into his pocket, George demands to see what he has. Lennie reveals that he is carrying a dead mouse—the first indication that Lennie enjoys petting soft things. George insists that Lennie hand over the mouse, and when he does, George throws it away.

George reminds Lennie that they are going to work at a ranch. Fearing that Lennie will reveal himself to be mentally deficient if he speaks, George tells Lennie not to say anything at the ranch. He also makes Lennie promise not to do any of the bad things that he did in Weed, the previous town in which they had worked. Lennie cannot remember what happened in Weed, but he does recall that he and George were run out of town.

As the sun goes down, George tells Lennie to gather firewood so they can heat up their dinner of canned beans. Lennie leaves but returns shortly carrying just one willow stick. Having observed the direction Lennie took, George correctly surmises that Lennie had retrieved the dead mouse he had thrown away. Once again George requires Lennie to hand over the lifeless creature so he can discard it. When George hurls the mouse far into the brush, Lennie starts to cry. George promises Lennie that he can pet a fresh mouse if he finds one. He sends Lennie out for firewood, and when the big man returns, George starts a fire and warms the beans.

As the beans are cooking, Lennie mentions that he likes ketchup with his beans. Knowing that they have no ketchup, George reacts furiously to this remark. It reminds him of all of Lennie's shortcomings and all of the sacrifices he has made for someone who is unable to appreciate them. George yells at Lennie, cursing him for his stupidity and telling him what a burden he has become. He upbraids him for the close call in Weed, revealing that the trouble occurred because Lennie tried to touch a young woman's dress to see how it felt. Frightened by the huge man's clumsy advance, the young woman mistakenly believed she was being assaulted and cried for help. Lennie and George had to flee, shrewdly hiding in an irrigation ditch. George ends his tirade abruptly.

After a pause, Lennie tells George that he "was only foolin'"[36] about the ketchup. He volunteers to go off into the woods so George can be alone. George apologizes for the outburst and asks Lennie not to leave. To show his goodwill, George promises to get Lennie a puppy to pet. The thought of the soft, furry animal prompts Lennie to ask George to tell him about owning rabbits. George agrees, and as the two men eat their beans, George recites a story of how he and Lennie will save up enough money to buy a ranch of their own and raise a cow, pigs, and rabbits. From time to time, Lennie breaks into the story, finishing George's sentences for him. Lennie's interruptions reveal that the story has been repeated many times and its recitation is a kind of ritual for the two men. The parts that Lennie remembers are significant, especially the sentence, "*I got you to look after me, and you got me to look after you,*"[37] which dramatizes the bond that has grown between the two men.

After rehearsing the dream about the ranch, George gives Lennie specific instructions about what to do in case he gets into trouble. He tells Lennie to come back to their campsite and hide in the brush. Lennie repeats the instructions, but George adds that Lennie must not get in any trouble or else he will not be allowed to tend the rabbits. Lennie understands. The chapter ends as the fire dies down and the two drifters retire for the night.

## The Ranch

The second chapter opens in the bunkhouse of the ranch. The crippled old ranch hand Candy leads George and Lennie into the room and points out their bunks. Lennie remains silent, but George and Candy make small talk about the ranch and the people who work there. Candy says that the boss is a "pretty nice fella" but sometimes gets "pretty mad."[38] He

*Gary Sinise (left) starred as George and John Malkovich (right) starred as Lennie in the 1992 film adaptation* Of Mice and Men.

reveals that the boss was unhappy that George and Lennie did not show up first thing in the morning. Soon the boss enters the bunkhouse and begins to question George and Lennie about why they were late for work. George does most of the talking, even answering questions directed at Lennie. The only comment Lennie makes is to repeat George's statement that he is "as strong as a bull."[39] The boss becomes suspicious of their conduct and finally asks George, "What stake have you got in this guy? You takin' his pay away from him?"[40] George assures the boss that he is not doing anything dishonest, just watching out for Lennie. The boss warns George that he will be keeping an eye on him, but that he can report to Slim's grain-threshing team.

After the boss leaves, George blames Lennie for having raised the boss's suspicions and almost costing them the job. George again tells Lennie not to speak. George notices that

Candy is just outside the door. Worried that Candy might be listening to his private conversation with Lennie, George confronts him. Candy reassures George that he was not listening. George accepts Candy's defense, and the two make small talk again until the boss's son, Curley, enters. Curley begins to ask Lennie questions, and George again answers on Lennie's behalf. This upsets Curley even more than it did his father. He demands that Lennie speak for himself, which Lennie does. After Curley leaves, George and Candy discuss the boss's son at length. Candy reveals that Curley is a former boxer who often picks fights with larger men. George remarks that he better leave Lennie alone. "This Curley punk is gonna get hurt if he messes around with Lennie,"[41] George states. As George begins to play solitaire with cards left on a small table, Candy tells him that Curley was recently married and keeps one hand in a glove filled with Vaseline to keep it soft for his wife. Candy describes Curley's wife as a flirt who seems attracted to several men on the ranch, especially Slim, the mule driver.

Sensing that Curley is a threat to their stay on the ranch, George warns Lennie to stay away from Curley. He repeats his instructions to meet by the pool in case anything bad happens. As the two are talking, Curley's wife enters the doorway of the bunkhouse. She asks George and Lennie if they have seen her husband. George answers that he was in the bunkhouse but has left. Curley's wife lingers in the doorway and talks with the new workers. George cuts her off, however, and she leaves. Seeing that Lennie was enthralled with the young woman, George sternly warns him to stay away from Curley's wife. Frightened by all the warnings, Lennie declares that he does not like the ranch and wants to leave. "This ain't no good place,"[42] he prophetically declares. George insists that they need to stay to make some money.

As George and Lennie are talking, the workers return from the field and begin to wash up for dinner. Slim enters the bunkhouse and greets George and Lennie. Slim asks George a few questions then states that he hopes George and Lennie are on his team. Like Curley and the boss, Slim notices that George does all of the talking and Lennie keeps quiet. He asks if the two men travel together. Unlike the questions from Curley and the boss, Slim's question seems friendly and sincere. George explains how he and Lennie "kinda look after each other."[43]

Carlson, another ranch hand, enters the bunkhouse, and Slim introduces him to George and Lennie. Carlson asks Slim about his dog's new pups. He suggests that Slim should convince Candy to shoot his old dog, which Carlson says stinks, and give him one of the pups. Before Slim responds, the dinner bell sounds and everyone but George and Lennie leaves. George assures Lennie that he will try to get one of the pups for him. Before the two head off to dinner, Curley returns to the bunkhouse and asks if either man has seen his wife. George says he saw her in the bunkhouse earlier, but she left. After Curley leaves, George tells Lennie that he hates Curley and just might end up getting into a fight with him.

## The Bunkhouse

The next chapter takes place later that evening in the bunkhouse. Slim and George enter the room together and talk. George thanks Slim for giving Lennie a puppy, and Slim states that he was impressed with Lennie's strength and hard work. With the other men pitching horseshoes in the yard, Slim again inquires about how the two men came to travel together. George tells him about how he knew Lennie's Aunt Clara and how he began to travel with him after she died. George confesses to Slim that traveling with Lennie is sometimes a burden and tells the team leader about the near disaster in Weed. Lennie enters the bunkhouse, and it is soon apparent that he has brought the puppy with him. George makes him return the puppy to the barn so it can be with its mother.

One by one the other workers file into the bunkhouse. Carlson again raises the subject of getting rid of Candy's dog because it stinks. When Candy refuses to shoot his dog, Carlson volunteers to do it for him. He tells Candy how he will shoot the dog at the base of the skull so that it will feel no pain. Candy still does not agree to put down his dog. Carlson appeals to Slim to promise one of his pups to Candy, which the mule driver does. Slim agrees with Carlson that the dog would probably be better off dead. Finally, Candy relents and Carlson leads the dog away. After a few agonizing minutes, a shot rings out. Heartbroken, Candy, who is lying on his bunk, turns toward the wall.

Crooks, the African American stable hand, enters the bunkhouse to tell Slim that he has warmed the tar that Slim wants to put on the hoof of one of the mules. After Slim goes out to the barn to tend to the mule, Carlson returns and begins cleaning his gun. Lennie also returns to the bunkhouse. Curley bursts in, again inquiring after his wife. Noticing that Slim is not in the bunkhouse, Curley asks where he is. When told that Slim has gone to the barn, Curley leaves abruptly. Sensing that a showdown is coming between Curley and Slim, some of the hands leave the bunkhouse to see what will happen. George and Lennie stay behind to avoid any kind of trouble. George asks Lennie if he saw Curley's wife in the barn before he left the pups. Lennie says she was not there, and George is satisfied that Slim did not go to the barn to meet Curley's wife.

Alone in the bunkhouse except for Candy, Lennie asks George to tell him about the place with the rabbits again. George again describes the ranch, embellishing the story with extra details. Candy overhears the entire story and asks George if he knows where a place like that might be. George is reluctant to discuss the plan with Candy but admits that he has a particular ranch in mind. When Candy asks how much the ranch might cost, George tells him that it would be about six hundred dollars. Candy then reveals that he has saved three hundred dollars and will have another fifty dollars at the end of the month. Worried that he might be cut from the ranch's payroll because of his age and his missing hand, Candy asks if he could go in with George and Lennie on the deal for the ranch. George is not sure he wants to let Candy in on his and Lennie's private dream, but he realizes that Candy's money could make the dream a reality. When Candy promises to leave his portion of the ranch to the other two when he dies, George agrees to take him on. Realizing that the "thing they had never really believed in was coming true,"[44] George, Lennie, and Candy grow silent with amazement.

The three men continue to elaborate on their dream, each getting more excited about their future. When George hears voices approaching the bunkhouse, he tells the other two men not to say anything about their plan to anyone else. Right before the other men return to the bunkhouse, Candy confesses

*Curley (center) confronts Lennie (right) as George looks on.*

to George that he should have shot his dog himself rather than letting someone else do it. The other hands enter the bunkhouse before George can respond to Candy, but the old man's words have a profound effect on George, who later will decide to take matters into his own hands regarding Lennie.

Slim, Curley, and the other hands enter the bunkhouse. Curley is in the midst of apologizing to Slim for once again asking him where his wife is. Slim warns Curley that he resents Curley's insinuations about him and Curley's wife and does not want to hear them anymore. Carlson chimes in that Curley needs to keep his wife under tighter control. Curley snaps at Carlson, telling him to keep his opinions to himself, but Carlson does not back down. He mocks Curley for having failed to intimidate Slim and calls him a coward. Carlson adds that he is not afraid of Curley either and will beat him badly if they ever fight. Sensing Curley's powerlessness, Candy expresses his disgust for Curley's "glove fulla vaseline."[45] Humiliated, Curley glances around the room and sees Lennie still smiling to himself about the dream of tending rabbits on the ranch.

Mistakenly believing that Lennie is smiling about his predicament, Curley launches an attack on the giant worker. Bewildered, Lennie does nothing to protect himself. Curley pummels him with blows to the face, drawing blood. Slim starts to intervene, but George stops him and tells Lennie to defend himself. At first Lennie does nothing, but with further urging he grabs Curley's fist in midair and crushes it in his hand. Curley writhes with pain, but the frightened Lennie does not release his hand until George is able to calm him down. Everyone realizes that the bones in Curley's hand are broken and that he will need to see a doctor. George asks Slim if he and Lennie will lose their jobs because of the fight. Slim kneels down by Curley and warns him not to try to get George and Lennie fired. If he does, Slim says that he will spread the word that Curley was beaten in a fight. Instead,

Curley is to say that his hand got caught in a machine. Curley agrees and leaves with Carlson to see a doctor. George tells Lennie that the fight was not his fault. Lennie asks George if he will still be able to tend the rabbits, and George assures him that he will.

## The Dream Grows

The fourth chapter takes place on Saturday night in Crooks's quarters, a tiny shed attached to the barn. Crooks is putting medicine on his back when Lennie appears at the doorway, drawn by the light in the room. Crooks tells Lennie that he is not welcome in his room and should leave. Lennie explains that everyone has left for town and that he has nothing to do. Crooks again tells Lennie to leave, but the large man lingers. Crooks finally invites Lennie to sit down, and the two men begin to talk. Lennie tells Crooks that Candy is in the bunkhouse with a pencil and paper making plans for the rabbits. When Crooks asks what rabbits Lennie is talking about, Lennie tells all about the ranch he, George, and Candy plan to buy. Crooks dismisses the idea as something that is "jus' in their head"[46] and will never actually happen. He suggests that George is just talking to pass the time. As he speaks to Lennie, Crooks realizes why the two men travel together. He points out how, because he is black, he is isolated from everyone else and is very lonely. He has books, but adds, "Books ain't no good. A guy needs somebody—to be near him. . . . Don't make no difference who the guy is, long's he's with you."[47]

Crooks hears Candy in the barn and gets up to see what he wants. When Candy says he is looking for Lennie, Crooks tells him that Lennie is in his room. He invites Candy in as well. Candy hesitates, but finally enters. After remarking what a nice room Crooks has, Candy begins to tell Lennie about his ideas about the rabbits. Crooks again dismisses the idea of the ranch as something that will never happen. When Candy tells him that he, George, and Lennie have picked out a place to buy and nearly have the money to do it, Crooks asks to join the enterprise.

Before Candy can respond to Crooks's offer, Curley's wife appears in the doorway of the room, asking for Curley. The three men say they have not seen Curley, but his wife surmises that he has gone to town with the other men to visit the prostitutes. Crooks and Candy are embarrassed by her presence, but Lennie is fascinated. Crooks tells Candy's wife to leave, but she does not. In a speech that parallels the one Crooks just gave, Curley's wife says she needs someone to talk with. She complains that Curley is not someone with whom she can really have a conversation. She asks if anyone knows what happened to Curley's hand. Candy tells her that it got caught in a machine, but Curley's wife sees through the lie. Candy tells her that she should leave and that no one is afraid of her or Curley anymore because they are planning to buy a place of their own. Curley's wife laughs at the idea, just as Crooks had moments before.

Noticing the bruises on Lennie's face, Curley's wife asks what happened to him. Not knowing what to say, Lennie states that Curley got his hand caught in a machine. Realizing that Lennie was the one who broke Curley's hand, Curley's wife says "O.K., Machine."[48] She makes a suggestive comment to Lennie, causing Crooks to demand that she leave. Curley's wife snaps at the black stable hand, reminding him that she could have him lynched simply by saying that he had attacked her sexually. Crooks instantly backs down, but Candy states that he would speak up for Crooks if she tried to tell a lie about him. Curley's wife tells Candy that no one would believe him, and he too backs down. Before she leaves, she thanks Lennie for hurting her husband because "he had it comin'."[49]

Returning from town, George seeks out Lennie. He scolds his large friend for being in Crooks's room. Crooks admits that he let Lennie visit because he is a nice person.

*Curley's wife (right) finds Lennie after he has killed a puppy and hidden it in the barn.*

Candy begins to tell George about his plans for the rabbits, but George cuts him short, reminding him not to talk about the plan in front of others. Candy apologizes, saying that he only told Crooks. As George, Lennie, and Candy begin to leave, Crooks tells Candy that he was "jus' foolin'" about wanting to be part of the ranch plans and that he "didn't mean it."[50]

## Disaster

As the fifth chapter opens, Lennie is sitting in the barn with his puppy, which is dead. Lennie scolds the lifeless animal for not being able to survive his play. Realizing that George will blame him for the puppy's death, Lennie begins to fear that he will not be allowed to tend the rabbits on the ranch. He becomes enraged at the puppy for dying and hurls it across the barn. He retrieves the dead pup and resumes talking to it.

Curley's wife enters the barn and approaches Lennie. The large man hides the dead puppy under some hay and tells the woman he is not allowed to speak to her. Curley's wife kneels down beside Lennie and tells him that she just wants to talk. "I never get to talk to nobody," she tells Lennie. "I get awful lonely."[51] Lennie resists, but Curley's wife asks what is under the hay. Lennie shows her the dead pup. Curley's wife is momentarily horrified but reassures Lennie that he will be able to get another pup.

Curley's wife tells Lennie that he should not be afraid to talk to her because she "ain't doin' no harm."[52] She begins to pour out her heart to Lennie, telling him about her unhappy marriage, the opportunities she passed up in the past, and how she still dreams of making something of herself. She describes her fantasy of becoming a movie starlet, which parallels Lennie and George's dream of one day owning a ranch.

Still afraid that he will get in trouble for killing the pup, Lennie repeats that he is worried he will not be able to tend the rabbits. When Curley's wife asks why Lennie is so interested in rabbits, Lennie tells her that he likes to touch them and other soft things. Curley's wife understands this simple desire and states that she likes to touch soft things as well. She and Lennie begin to discuss the feel of materials such as silk and velvet. Curley's wife reveals that she likes to make her hair soft by brushing it and invites Lennie to feel it. Lennie touches the young woman's hair and is entranced by its texture. Curley's wife tells Lennie not to mess up her hair, but Lennie strokes it harder. Curley's wife pulls away, but Lennie holds on to her hair. Curley's wife shouts at Lennie, demanding that he release her. When Curley's wife screams, Lennie realizes that he may get into trouble with George. He covers Curley's wife's mouth and nose with his hand and pleads with her to be quiet. Terrified, Curley's wife tries to free herself from the large man's grip. Convinced that George will not let him tend rabbits if he finds out about the struggle in the barn, Lennie begs Curley's wife to stop fighting him. He moves his hand away from her mouth for a moment, but when she cries out again he gets angry. "Don't you go yellin'," he commands, then gives her a shake. With his tremendous strength, Lennie accidentally snaps the woman's neck. When he realizes that he has done "a bad thing,"[53] Lennie decides he must leave and hide in the brush by the pool.

Candy eventually enters the barn and discovers the lifeless body of Curley's wife. Rather than shout for help, Candy finds George and brings him to the scene of the mishap. George concludes that Lennie must have killed the woman. Candy suggests that they should give Lennie time to escape, but George believes they need to find him and turn him in to the authorities since Lennie could never survive on his own. Candy warns George that Curley will want to lynch Lennie, but George continues to believe that everyone needs to know what happened. Candy asks George if the mishap will affect their plans for the ranch. George confirms Candy's worst fears. "I think I knowed we'd never do her,"[54] he says.

Worried that the other hands might think he had something to do with the death of Curley's wife, George tells Candy to wait a few minutes before telling everyone what happened so that he has time to go back to the bunkhouse. Candy obeys, then retrieves the other workers. Curley instantly surmises that Lennie is to blame for the incident. As Candy predicted, Curley calls for vengeance and leads an armed band of men to hunt Lennie down and kill him. George pleads with Curley to capture Lennie alive, but Curley scoffs at the suggestion. George appeals to Slim, but the mule driver points out that taking Lennie alive could lead to his being strapped down and put "in a cage."[55] Nevertheless, Slim tries to dissuade Curley from joining the manhunt. When Curley refuses, Slim instructs Candy to stay behind with the body of Curley's wife, and all of the other men leave. Alone with the corpse, Candy upbraids the dead woman for causing all of the trouble and for destroying the dream of buying a ranch.

## An Act of Mercy

The final chapter opens in the same place that the story began: the green pool. Lennie enters the clearing from the brush, kneels down, and drinks from the pool as he did before. He sits in the clearing and talks to himself about how angry George is going to be. Lennie envisions his Aunt Clara standing before him, scolding him for not listening to George and for being a burden to him. Lennie then imagines that a large rabbit is standing in front of him. The rabbit also scolds Lennie for his misdeed and accuses him of being unable to

*George (standing) comforts Lennie just before he shoots him.*

tend the rabbits carefully. Lennie covers his ears and calls for George, who enters from the brush.

Lennie expects George to yell at him for doing a bad thing, but George says that Lennie's actions "make no difference."[56] Lennie offers, as he did in the first chapter, to go off and live in a cave, but George tells Lennie that he wants him to stay. Lennie asks to hear about the rabbits again, and George begins the familiar story. When George is unable to finish the sentence about how he has Lennie and Lennie has him, Lennie completes the sentence for him. George tells Lennie to take off his hat and look across the river. As George continues the story, he draws Carlson's Luger pistol out of his jacket, releases the safety, and holds it behind Lennie. As the voices of the other men approach, George raises the gun but is unable to use it. He continues telling Lennie about the rabbits as the men come nearer. Lennie asks if George is mad at him. George tells him that he has never been mad. "That's one thing I want ya to know,"[57] he says. As the ranch hands crash through the brush nearby, George points the gun at the base of Lennie's skull and pulls the trigger. Lennie dies instantly.

When the ranch hands reach the clearing, they surmise that Lennie had Carlson's gun and that George had wrestled it away from him and shot him in self-defense. George agrees with this account. Slim alone guesses the truth. He takes George by the elbow and assures him that he did the right thing. Slim leads George away and promises to buy him a drink. The uncomprehending Carlson watches the two men move away and asks, "Now what the hell ya suppose is eatin' them two guys?"[58]

# CHAPTER FOUR

# The Cast
# of Characters

Although some critics have accused Steinbeck of filling *Of Mice and Men* with unreal, subhuman, and mechanical characters, most critics and readers find the cast of characters to be entirely believable and even memorable. Many of the characters are misfits in one way or another: Lennie is retarded, Candy is crippled, Crooks is part of a racial minority, Curley's wife is the lone woman on the ranch. Except for the ranch owner, his son, and his son's wife, all of the characters belong to the lowest class of workers. Many are homeless, living in the ranch bunkhouse with no place of their own.

### George Milton

An itinerant worker, George travels from ranch to ranch trying to earn enough money to build up a stake, a sum of money great enough to allow him to change his lifestyle. Small of stature, George is strong for his size and

*George, portrayed here by Gary Sinise, is a ranch hand who empathizes with others.*

quick-witted. He also shows a great deal more compassion for his fellow human beings than most of the other ranch hands do. In particular, he cares for, entertains, and protects his feebleminded traveling companion, Lennie, who clearly would be lost in the harsh world of migrant labor without George's help.

George's relationship with Lennie raises suspicions in the minds of many of the people the two drifters meet. When the ranch boss asks George and Lennie a series of questions, George answers on behalf of both men, prompting the boss to ask, "What are you tryin' to put over?"[59] The boss pointedly asks George if he is taking Lennie's pay and warns him not to try anything underhanded. The boss's son, Curley, also wants to know why George answers questions directed at Lennie. "What the hell are you gettin' into it for?" Curley asks George. When George replies that he and Lennie travel together, Curley remarks suggestively, "Oh, so it's that way." George ignores the implication of anything improper and replies, "Yeah, it's that way."[60]

George tends to keeps his distance from the other workers and is slow to join in conversations. When he plays cards, he almost always plays solitaire, a game for one. He is not a complete loner, however. He tells Slim about the trouble he and Lennie got into in Weed. He also tells Candy about his and Lennie's dream of buying their own ranch and settling down. George's willingness to confide in others suggests that his standoffish behavior is not an expression of his true nature but a strategy to shelter Lennie from attention.

Despite George's best efforts to shield his friend from the dangers of the world, catastrophe finally catches up to Lennie in the form of Curley's lonely and flirtatious wife. When George discovers Lennie's deadly blunder, he realizes that he cannot allow his friend to suffer the tortuous death that Curley has vowed to inflict on him. In his final act as Lennie's guardian, George summons the strength to end his friend's life as painlessly as possible.

## Lennie Small

A huge man, Lennie Small seems comically misnamed. "He ain't very small,"[61] Carlson jokes when Lennie is introduced to him by his full name. The contrast between Lennie's surname and his size serves to dramatize his imposing physical presence.

*Small* applies to everything about Lennie except his size—his mental capacity, his interests, his hopes, and his dreams. George freely admits to both Slim and the boss that Lennie is not bright. This is an understatement. Lennie is severely mentally impaired. He cannot remember the simplest commands and reacts to the world in a childlike, sometimes infantile way. "Look, George. Look what I done,"[62] Lennie cries when he makes rings in a pond with his fingers. He can barely contain his excitement when he hears that Slim's dog has had puppies. When he receives a puppy of his own, Lennie lies down in the barn with it and even tries to sneak it into his bunk at night.

Lennie's main interest in life is to find things that are soft to touch. He pets a dead mouse that he has found because

*Lennie caresses the soft hair of Curley's wife because he loves to touch soft things.*

he likes the feel of its fur. He strokes the puppy he received from Slim from head to tail even after he accidentally kills it. Lennie's obsession with tactile stimulation caused the near disaster in Weed, where his desire to touch a girl's dress was misinterpreted as an attempted rape, and it leads to the catastrophe with Curley's wife.

Lennie's hopes for the future revolve around his tactile fixation. He shares George's dream of settling down on a ranch mainly because it means that he will be able to tend the many rabbits they plan to raise. "What makes you so nuts about rabbits?" asks Curley's wife when Lennie tells her about the ranch he and George plan to buy. "I like to pet nice things," Lennie explains. "Once at a fair I seen some of them long-hair rabbits. An' they was nice, you bet."[63]

When Lennie perceives that the cries of Curley's wife may cost him the job of tending rabbits, he acts swiftly to defend his treasured dream. He covers the young woman's mouth and nose with his large hand to stifle her screams. "George gonna say I done a bad thing," Lennie tells the struggling woman. "He ain't gonna let me tend no rabbits."[64] When Curley's wife continues to thrash about under his hold, Lennie gives her a shake to make her stop, inadvertently breaking her neck in the process. Lennie's compulsion to touch things is a defect of his nature, but his decision to silence Curley's wife, though dimwitted, is deliberate, motivated by his desire to save his dream of tending rabbits.

## Curley's Wife

Curley's wife is a minority of one—the only female on the ranch. She is also the only character without a name, a fact that reinforces her status as a person at the margins of the society in which she lives. She is identified only as the wife of Curley, as if she is his possession.

Isolated in the all-male world of the ranch, Curley's wife desperately seeks human contact. Because she is young, at-

*George warns Curley's wife of the trouble she could cause on the ranch.*

tractive, and flirtatious, she awakens the desires of many of the men, causing them to react strongly to her presence. Most become angry, fearing that any kind of involvement with her might lead to their dismissal since she is married to the boss's son. Others talk about her behind her back with a mixture of admiration and disgust. Only Lennie, who is oblivious to her sexual innuendo, is willing to look directly at her and speak to her openly.

Sensing Lennie's childlike innocence, Curley's wife feels safe with him and tells him all about her past—how she "coulda made somethin'" of herself and perhaps "will yet."[65] She relates how a Hollywood producer had once told her she was a natural and promised to put her in the motion pictures. She describes her dream of being a movie actress with the same careful detail that George and Lennie use to describe their ranch. Her dream serves the same function as George and Lennie's: It gives her hope for the future and a momentary escape from the present.

Curley's wife is the only person who attempts to understand Lennie's interest in touching soft things. In her desire for human contact, she makes small talk about the texture of things such as silk and velvet. For the first time Lennie is involved in a conversation about what matters to him. "Do you like to feel velvet?" Curley's wife asks. "You bet, by God,"[66] Lennie cries. Swept up in this moment of human contact, Curley's wife invites Lennie to touch her hair, a softness that is important to her, one that she cultivates by brushing her hair. Lennie touches her hair, but this moment of seemingly innocent contact ultimately proves fatal to both Curley's wife and Lennie.

## Candy

An elderly worker who lost one of his hands in a work-related accident, Candy has been reduced to performing the most menial jobs on the ranch, such as cleaning the bunkhouse. Because of his advanced age and his physical disability, Candy

*Candy (left), portrayed by Ray Walston, has a subservient job on the ranch and worries that he will no longer be needed.*

senses that his usefulness on the ranch is waning and worries that he soon will be dropped from the payroll.

Concerned about his future, Candy is intrigued by George's description of the farm that he and Lennie dream of owning. He asks George if he might be allowed to join in the venture. George is reluctant to admit the outsider into his and Lennie's private scheme. "You got nothin' to do with us,"[67] George tells the old man. When Candy reveals that he has more than half of the money needed to buy the ranch George has in mind, George softens toward him.

Although Candy appears on the surface to be one of the weakest figures on the ranch, his secret bankroll gives him unexpected power. George calculates that with Candy's savings and his and Lennie's earnings, the three men "could swing" a deal to buy a ranch within a month. Through Candy, the plan that George "had never really believed in" was "coming true." This realization creates a high point of the novel, a moment of transcendent peace when the three men "fell into silence" and "sat still, all bemused by the beauty of the thing."[68]

Despite Lennie's mental deficiencies, Candy treats him like an equal, twice seeking him out to share further plans about raising rabbits. The second time Candy searches for Lennie, he goes to the barn where Lennie often plays with his puppy. It is there that Candy discovers the lifeless body of Curley's wife. Rather than tell everyone about the mishap, Candy finds George and secretly brings him to the barn. Candy's act of loyalty toward his partners allows George enough time to take Carlson's pistol from the bunkhouse and form his plan for how to deal with Lennie.

## Slim

A highly skilled mule team driver, Slim commands the respect of everyone on the ranch. Tall and self-confident, Slim moves about the ranch "with a majesty only achieved by royalty and master craftsmen."[69] When he speaks, others fall silent. Nearly

*Slim (center) looks at Lennie (right) as George tells him to put the puppy away.*

everyone looks to him for advice. When Slim agrees with Carlson that Candy's old dog would be better off dead, Candy looks at Slim helplessly "for Slim's opinions were law."[70]

Slim's thoughtful and friendly demeanor "invited confidence without demanding it."[71] George not only explains to Slim why he and Lennie travel together, but he also tells him about the events in Weed. Slim keeps these confidences to himself but later acts on his conclusion that Lennie "ain't a bit mean"[72] by standing up for the oafish giant when he grabs Curley's hand in self-defense and crushes it. Slim warns Curley not to tell anyone that Lennie had hurt him and not to attempt to fire Lennie or George from their jobs, otherwise he will spread the word that Curley lost a fight "an' then will you get the laugh."[73] Curley sullenly agrees not to tell.

Because of his insight into George and Lennie's relationship, Slim is the only character to see through George's suggestion that he shot Lennie in self-defense. Knowing the bond that existed between the two drifters, Slim instantly realizes that George executed Lennie out of compassion. Slim reassures George that he did the right thing, stating, "You hadda, George. I swear you hadda."[74] He leads George away from the scene after the shooting with the promise of further comfort over a drink.

## Carlson

A heavyset ranch hand, Carlson is tough, impatient, and insensitive to the wants and needs of those around him. Offended by the smell of Candy's old dog, Carlson suggests that Candy put the dog down. When Candy refuses to kill his old friend, Carlson persists, arguing that the dog would be better off dead. When Candy admits that he would be afraid of hurting the animal, Carlson offers to shoot the dog himself. He even draws Slim into the discussion, getting the highly respected mule driver to promise one of his dog's puppies to Candy. Slim sides with Carlson, honestly believing that killing the dog would be the humane thing to do. Although Carlson argues the same point, it is clear that he does so not out of compassion for the dog but simply as a means to get what he wants. After Candy relents, Carlson leads the old dog away and shoots him.

When Curley's wife is found dead, Carlson eagerly takes up a shotgun to hunt down Lennie. Carlson shows no qualms about following Curley's instructions to shoot Lennie in the stomach, suggesting that he shares Curley's sadistic streak. When Slim comforts George after he has shot Lennie, the self-centered Carlson does not comprehend the bond that has formed between the two men. "Now what the hell ya suppose is eatin' them two guys?"[75] he asks.

## Crooks

Like Curley's wife, Crooks is a minority of one—the only African American on the ranch. Crooks does not share quarters with the other ranch hands; he is segregated in the harness room, a shed connected to the barn. "I ain't wanted in the bunk house," Crooks tells Lennie. When the uncomprehending Lennie asks why, Crooks answers, "'Cause I'm black."[76]

Though advanced in years and partially crippled, Crooks is a knowledgeable and capable stable hand. Because he has lived on the ranch a long time, Crooks has acquired more personal possessions than the other hands. He keeps several books and magazines in his room, a sign that he is better read than most of the ranch hands.

Crooks keeps his room clean and neat, prompting Candy to remark, "You got a nice cozy little place in here."[77] Crooks is quick to point out that his room is not as idyllic as it seems since the manure pile is located under his window. The location of the manure pile is a reminder of the low regard in which Crooks is held because of his race.

A proud man, Crooks has no illusions about being on an equal footing with the whites on the ranch. All it takes is a word from Curley's wife to silence him when he demands that she leave his room. "You know what I can do to you if you open your trap," Curley's wife warns Crooks. "Yes, ma'am,"[78] Crooks replies, knowing that the word of a white woman would be enough to have him lynched.

Although he is determined to keep his distance from white people, Crooks cannot resist the power and beauty of George, Lennie, and Candy's dream of owning a ranch. After first dismissing their scheme as nothing more than a fantasy, the old stable hand changes his mind after hearing from Candy that the three men nearly have the money to carry out their plan. Caught up by the idea, Crooks asks if he might join the enterprise, saying, "If you . . . guys would want a hand to work for nothing—just his keep, why I'd come and lend a hand."[79] After Curly's wife threatens him, and George criticizes Candy for telling Crooks about the plan to buy a ranch, Crooks withdraws his offer to help. "I didn't mean it. Jus' foolin'. I wouldn't want to go to no place like that,"[80] he says.

## Curley

Mean-spirited and angry, Curley is a troublemaker who probably would be dismissed from the ranch were it not for the fact that his father is the boss. Small in stature and insecure about his sexual prowess, Curley feels compelled to constantly prove his masculinity by verbally and physically abusing those around him.

Curley's name, or nickname, is derived from the fact that he has tightly curled hair—not a masculine physical trait. His boots are described as "high-heeled," a term that suggests that they are designed to fit in the stirrups of a saddle but also connotes a woman's shoe. The high heels also help Curley appear taller. In contrast, the tall and self-confident Slim is described as "not needing high-heeled boots."[81]

Curley's anxiety about his masculinity is heightened by the fact that he has recently married the attractive young woman who is identified simply as his wife. Although her name—or the lack thereof—connotes that she is Curley's possession, at times it appears the other way around—she possesses and controls Curley. While his wife moves freely about the ranch, chatting and flirting with the ranch hands, Curley races from place to place in search of her. He has filled the one leather glove that he wears with Vaseline in order to soften it for his wife. Curley has adopted this curious practice either at the suggestion of his wife, who may have found his hands too rough, or out of his own desperate need to please her. Either way, the glove symbolizes Curley's insecurity over his manhood and at the same time further feminizes him.

Because he is an accomplished boxer who is willing and even eager to fight, Curley is able to intimidate most of the ranch hands. Because of his size and strength, Lennie is not particularly afraid of Curley; he is more afraid of angering

George and jeopardizing his role as caretaker of the rabbits. When Curley provokes and even attacks Lennie, the big man does not fight back out of fear of upsetting George. When Curley bloodies Lennie, George gives his giant friend permission to defend himself. Lennie simply seizes Curley's fist and crushes it in his giant hand.

Warned by Slim not to retaliate against Lennie and George by having them fired, Curley exacts no revenge for his injury, but he clearly carries a grudge against the huge worker. Later, when he discovers that Lennie has killed his wife, Curley vows to "get" Lennie by shooting him "in the guts,"[82] which would be a slow and painful method of execution. George pleads with Curley not to shoot Lennie, explaining that the big man is "nuts" and "di'n't know what he was doin'."[83] Curley scoffs at the suggestion, arguing that Lennie has armed himself with Carlson's Luger. Slim suggests Curley's real motive is revenge, stating, "Curley's still mad about his hand."[84] Although Slim and the others would be willing to capture Lennie and send him to jail or an asylum for the criminally insane, Curley is determined to kill him. Knowing this, George chooses to end Lennie's life humanely. Curley's lust for vengeance is the driving force behind Lennie's death.

CHAPTER FIVE

# Critical Analysis

riting to his agents, John Steinbeck described *Of Mice and Men* as a microcosm—a small world, or community, that represents a larger one. The book is indeed small—approximately one hundred pages in most editions. The story takes place in just four locations: a clearing by a pool, the bunkhouse of a ranch, the room of a stable hand, and a barn. The plot is simple: Two men come to a ranch to work; one man inadvertently kills a young woman; the other man kills him. These are the small things, but what is the large thing? What, if anything, does the story stand for? Steinbeck arranged the speech and images to suggest many things at once, and critics of the book have found the seemingly simple story to be rich in themes and symbolism.

## A Social Conflict

When John Steinbeck wrote *Of Mice and Men,* the United States and the rest of the industrialized world were in the eighth year of the Great Depression, the worst financial crisis of modern times. The value of the New York Stock Exchange had plummeted by more than $50 billion, tens of thousands of businesses had failed, manufacturing output had dropped by half, and millions of people were out of work. Rather than

*A migrant worker irrigates a field in California. The plots of* The Grapes of Wrath *and* Of Mice and Men *were inspired by the lives of migrant farmers.*

face constant unemployment in the cities, many people took to the road, hoping to find work on the farms and ranches that continued to produce food for the nation, though at greatly reduced prices.

Against this backdrop of economic hardship, the plight of George and Lennie took on special meaning. Theirs was not a romantic tale far removed from everyday life; for many Americans, theirs was everyday life. Those who had not gone on the road themselves at least knew of others who had. *Of Mice and Men* gave them a snapshot of life as a bindle stiff, or hobo.

It also portrays the differences between the "haves" and "have-nots" of society. George and Lennie are members of that lowest of classes now frequently described as the working poor. They aspire to earn enough money to buy a ranch of their own and enjoy the fruits of their labor, but they have managed to save only about $10. When they join up with Candy, who received $250 as a settlement for losing his hand in a ranching accident, their dream of becoming land-owners becomes plausible. They are thwarted in their efforts by Curley, who attained his position in the upper class by birth rather than by hard work. "Society proves too strong," writes critic B. Ramachandra Rao. "The society is represented by the ranch-owner's son, Curley, whose arrogance is supported by the social system which gives no chance at all for the underdog. It is this society with its complex structure which gives a new dimension to the struggles of the Steinbeck hero."[85]

## Self-Help

As the depression swept through the country, a national debate arose over the proper way of dealing with the crisis. Many people believed that the federal government should stimulate the economy and take action to assist those in need. Others, including President Herbert Hoover, disagreed. They believed that the national strengths that had created the booming economy of the 1920s would eventually return the nation to prosperity. In February 1931 Hoover declared,

> This is not an issue as to whether people shall go hungry or cold in the United States. It is solely a question of the best method by which hunger and cold shall be prevented. It is a question of whether the American people . . . will maintain the spirit of charity and mutual self-help . . . as distinguished . . . from appropriations out of the Federal Treasury for such purposes. . . . I am confident that our people have the resources, the initiative, the courage, the stamina and the kindliness of spirit to meet this situation in the way they have met their problems over generations.[86]

Millions of people agreed with Hoover. They believed that hard work and initiative would overcome any obstacle, even the Great Depression. Some even saw the hard times as an opportunity. Since it took greater efforts than usual to succeed in a depression, these optimists believed that those who worked the hardest had a better chance than usual to get ahead. "Many of us learned in the Depression how to turn a disadvantage into an advantage," says salesman W. Clement Stone. "A person doesn't have to be poor." The key to success, Stone maintains, "is known as PMA, positive mental attitude."[87] Henry Ford, the founder of the Ford Motor Company, agreed that average people could succeed through self-help. He believed that the best remedy for unemployment was to turn to the land. "No unemployment insurance can be compared to an alliance between a man and a plot of land," Ford wrote at the time. "Let every man and every family at this season of the year cultivate a plot of land and raise a sufficient supply for themselves or others. . . . Groups of men could rent farms for small sums and operate them on the co-operative plan."[88]

In some ways, *Of Mice and Men* dramatizes the futility of Ford's self-help plan. Lennie and George envision owning a plot and becoming self-sufficient. They definitely have a positive mental attitude. Everyone else in the story scoffs at the idea that they could ever buy their own ranch, but Lennie and George have the strength of purpose to hold fast to their dream. With Candy's entry into the scheme, it looks for a moment as if the three men will prove Ford right. The plan unravels, however, when Lennie is not able to control his private urges and almost superhuman strength. It is as if Steinbeck, who believed in a nonteleological universe—one in which events occur without any grand purpose—was satirizing the whole notion of self-help and positive mental attitude.

## Friendship and Commitment

While some critics believe that *Of Mice and Men* represents the struggle of an entire class or group, others find the richness of the book to be in the relationship between George and Lennie. As simple as the relationship appears to be, no one on the ranch seems to understand it. The boss, Candy, Curley, and Slim all display confusion at the fact that George and Lennie travel together. They all ask George what is behind the unique arrangement. George's answer varies depending on who asks the question, but it usually involves the notion that George has promised Lennie's family to watch out for him.

The truth is much simpler, of course, and is summed up in a line from the story that George and Lennie recite throughout the book: *"Because I got you to look after me, and you got me to look after you."*[89] Friendship conquers the isolation that is the natural condition of everyone in the book. Nearly every character expresses a desire to have the kind of relationship that Lennie and George have. "A guy needs somebody—to be near him,"[90] says Crooks. The problem is that true friendship is not easy to maintain. It requires patience, forgiveness, and self-sacrifice—all of which are required of George and Lennie.

The ultimate test of friendship comes at the end of the book, when George must summon all of his strength to do the best thing for his friend. Critic Louis Owens maintains that George's final act of mercy is genuinely heroic: "In accepting complete responsibility for Lennie, George demonstrates the degree of commitment necessary to the Steinbeck hero, and in fact enters the ranks of those heroes."[91]

## The Arthurian Legend

Some critics believe that George's heroism arises not only from his friendship

*The tales of King Arthur (pictured) and the knights of the Round Table inspired Steinbeck.*

with Lennie but out of a sense of honor and duty handed down through the ages from medieval knights. As a boy, Steinbeck was fascinated with the story of King Arthur and the knights of the Round Table. As an adult, Steinbeck continued to be inspired by the Arthurian legend. "Tortilla Flat grew out of my study of the Arthurian cycle," he wrote in an introduction to a collection of his short novels. "I wanted to take the stories of my town of Monterey and cast them into a kind of folklore."[92] Later in life, Steinbeck spent five years translating Malory's *Le Morte D'Arthur*. *Of Mice and Men* also borrows several elements from the legend of Arthur. The story involves a fraternity of men who are inspired by a common dream, as the knights of the Round Table were. George, Lennie, and Candy show an uncommon loyalty for each other that is reminiscent of the allegiance between the Arthurian knights. George commits his life to helping Lennie almost as if he had taken the knight's pledge to defend the powerless. Like Camelot, the dream of a ranch proves too fragile for this fallen world, but the love and fellowship of the men who dreamed it remain an inspiration.

## The Power of Dreams

George and Lennie's dream of one day owning a ranch functions almost like a character in the drama, appearing in five of the six chapters of the book. Like a living creature, the dream is born, it grows, and it dies. It affects the lives of nearly everyone who hears about it, giving them purpose and hope. The dream is larger than any one character, and perhaps is larger than any one dream. Lennie's description of his dream of tending rabbits awakens Curley's wife's own dream of being a movie star. As she and Lennie contemplate their dreams side by side, the two dreams seem to merge into one human hope.

The dream represents different things to the different dreamers. Candy sees owning his own ranch as a way to gain the security in old age that working on a ranch cannot provide. George sees it as a way to gain independence, to work for himself rather than for others. It represents a way to gain control over his daily life. With his own place, George believes he will have the freedom to work as he pleases. He will not have to answer to others. The ranch also offers freedom to Lennie—endless freedom to touch soft animals. The ranch will also provide Lennie a haven from the confusing world of migrant labor, a safe place where he can be with George. Crooks sees the ranch as a place where he can gain respect. Curley's wife's dream offers her human contact—a chance to meet with reporters, have her picture taken, speak into a microphone to a public that will listen. For all of the dreamers, the dream represents a chance to experience a sense of self-respect and dignity that is not available on the ranch where they currently live.

Each character understands that he or she will have to make sacrifices and overcome hardships to make the dream come true. Lennie is acutely aware that in order to attain his dream he must avoid doing bad things. George needs to manage things so that he and Lennie keep their jobs long enough to earn the money they need to buy the ranch. He cannot afford to waste money drinking, gambling, or carousing. Candy must sacrifice his life's savings to fulfill the dream. Crooks has to overcome his cynicism and his mistrust of white people. Curley's wife will have to leave Curley.

Even these sacrifices will not ensure that the dream comes true. Obstacles appear. Some come from outside powers. Curley's violent temper is a threat to his wife, to Lennie, and even to George and Candy. Lennie's unpredictable behavior threatens the dream for George. Other obstacles lie within the characters themselves. Curley's wife's need for closeness poses a danger to her dream, and Lennie's uncontrollable strength and his tactile compulsion pose a danger to his. In the end, the characters in *Of Mice and Men* are not able to overcome these obstacles, but that does not mean that all dreams are unattainable, only that their achievement is unpredictable and may involve forces beyond human control.

## Fate

Steinbeck originally titled his novella-drama *Something That Happened* to emphasize that the author was not passing judgment on the events he depicts. Steinbeck credited his friend Edward Ricketts, a marine biologist, with helping him develop a nonjudgmental approach to the depiction

*Robert Burns wrote a poem that inspired the title of* Of Mice and Men.

of characters and situations. Apparently, however, *Something That Happened* was a bit too bloodless of a title, even for the scientist Ricketts, for it was Ricketts who suggested that the book be called *Of Mice and Men*.

Ricketts drew the title from a poem by the Scottish poet Robert Burns titled "To a Mouse On Turning Her Up in Her Nest with a Plow." Seeing that he has accidentally destroyed the creature's carefully built home, the poet notes how

The best laid schemes o' mice an' men
Gang aft a-gley [often go awry]
An' lea'e us nought but grief and pain
For promis'd joy.[93]

By alluding to these lines, the title draws attention to the unpredictable nature of life. All living creatures—from mice to human beings—are at the mercy of forces beyond their control. People may believe that their destiny is in their own hands, but this is an illusion. Lennie, George, and especially

Candy lay their plans with great care, but their scheme unravels when Lennie and Curley's wife meet in the barn and the fatal events occur.

The ancient Greeks believed that people who acted as though they were in control of their destiny risked offending the gods, who would punish them for their hubris, or overconfidence. As Candy begins to believe that the dream of owning a ranch is going to come true, he begins to revel in his newfound independence. Bolstered by the belief that he soon will not need his job on the ranch, Candy angrily demands that Curley's wife leave Crooks's room. He tells the young woman that he, Lennie, and Crooks are not afraid of her anymore. "Maybe there was a time when we was scared of gettin' canned, but we ain't no more," the old man tells her. "We got our lan', and it's ours, an' we c'n go to it."[94] His outburst is a minor act of hubris, but he pays dearly for it nevertheless.

The classic concept of fate suggests that events occur to test character, but the outcome of these conflicts are not predestined. To an extent, a person's fate lies within his or her character. Lennie's tragic flaw is his inability to control his impulses, a trait that is apparent in the first scene of the book. As soon as George recounts the events in Weed, a sense of doom pervades the story. It seems like only a matter of time until Lennie repeats his mistake, and it is. Fate brings him together with Curley's wife in the barn, but the result of this meeting lies within Lennie's character. The same is true for Curley's wife, whose tragic flaw is her disregard for the dangers of pursuing human contact.

## Good and Evil

Not all of the conflicts faced by the characters in *Of Mice and Men* come from within themselves. They also must deal with people around them whose intentions are not always good. Indeed, early critics of the book assailed the story for being an oversimplified struggle between good and evil. In this reading, the compassionate George and the innocent Lennie are good while the belligerent Curley and his flirtatious wife are bad. The conflicts between these forces are the focus of the book. At one point the good Lennie crushes the hand of the bad Curley. Later Curley's bad wife succeeds in getting the good Lennie to break his promise not to talk to her. In the end, the good George mercifully destroys the good Lennie to prevent his horrible death at hands of the evil Curley.

Steinbeck is concerned with good and evil, but lines between them are often blurred. For example, most critics view Slim as the epitome of goodness in the book. Steinbeck describes him as the "prince of the ranch" whose "authority was so great that his word was taken on any subject."[95] Slim offers to defend Lennie from Curley in the middle of the book. Likewise, he alone understands what George has done at the end of the book and extends compassion to him.

But Slim rarely uses his power as a force for good. If he is a god, he is an indifferent one. For example, when Carlson attempts to bully Candy into shooting his dog, the powerless old swamper appeals to Slim for help, but Slim gives him none. Later, when Lennie is attacked by Curley, Slim talks about stopping the fight but actually does nothing. Most crucially, when Curley's wife is found dead, George appeals to Slim to stop Curley from killing Lennie. Slim's attempt to deter Curley is pathetically weak. "Curley—maybe you better stay here with your wife," Slim says. Curley recognizes the half-hearted remark for what it is. "I'm goin',"[96] he declares emphatically. When Curley and Slim are headed for a showdown, Whit, one of the other hands, says that Curley should leave Slim alone because "nobody don't know what Slim can do."[97] By the end of the book it is clear why no one knows what Slim can do: He has never done anything. His unwillingness to help anyone makes Slim more of a force of evil than of good.

Everyone on the ranch talks about Curley as if he is evil incarnate, but here again the facts are ambiguous. Early in the book Curley asks Lennie a direct question, but George answers. Curley tells George to let Lennie talk, a demand that is not really that outrageous. In the heated exchange that follows, George is at least equally to blame for the bitter words, if not more so. After Curley leaves, Candy and George continue to discuss him until George finally concludes that he hates the boss's son. Later, when Curley lashes out at Lennie, it is seen as a completely evil act. Right before the attack, however, everyone in the group had been belittling Curley. Carlson had called him a coward, and Candy had derided him for putting Vaseline in his glove. When Curley looked at Lennie, all he saw was a smile on the big man's face. He had no way of knowing that Lennie was thinking of his private fantasy about the rabbit ranch. Though not justified, Curley's attack is at least understandable.

Curley's wife is not completely evil, either. She is revealed to be one of the most isolated and lonely people on the ranch. As a result, her flirtatious behavior can be seen as a desperate and misguided attempt to gain the affection and attention she needs. Although she manipulates the mentally helpless Lennie into breaking his promise not to speak to her, the punishment she receives for this action—death—hardly seems fitting.

Lennie often is seen as a good-hearted person whose death at the end of the book evokes the mixture of pity and awe known as catharsis, which is the goal of tragedy. George spends a great deal of time telling others that Lennie is stupid but not mean. George must convince everyone that despite his size Lennie is not a threat, otherwise he and Lennie may lose their jobs. However, George is being less than honest about Lennie's true nature.

If the reader ignores George's statements about Lennie and judges the large man on his actions alone, his goodness appears rather ambiguous. Within the two-day time span of the story, Lennie crushes Curley's hand, kills a puppy, and kills a woman. Mark Van Doren accurately observes that

"Lennie is a half-witted giant with a passion for petting mice—or rabbits, or pups, or girls—and for killing them when they don't like it."[98] Although Lennie seems to like animals, the truth is that he sees them as objects. When they assert their animal nature, he destroys them. He confesses to George that he killed his pet mice when they bit him, and he tells Curley's wife that he killed the pup when it looked as if the pup were going to bite him. As critic Leo Gurkos points out, it does not matter much to Lennie whether the things he pets are dead or alive. "He draws no distinction between life and death," Gurkos writes. "He extracts as much pleasure in stroking a dead mouse as a live one."[99]

Lennie objectifies Curley's wife as well. When she struggles for her life, he shows no concern for her. Instead, he becomes angry and gives her a shake to silence her. His motive for silencing the woman is purely selfish: He does not want to forfeit his opportunity to tend rabbits when he and George buy their ranch.

Steinbeck's goal is not to pass judgment on any of the characters; rather, he wishes to reveal that no person is wholly good or wholly bad but a subtle and ever-changing mixture of both.

*Lennie gasps in horror after he has accidentally killed Curley's wife.*

## Cain and Abel

One of the oldest stories of good and evil appears in the first book of the Bible. It is the tale of Cain and Abel. Many critics contend that *Of Mice and Men* is a variation on the ancient biblical story. These critics point out that many years after publishing *Of Mice and Men,* Steinbeck wrote another novel based on the Cain-and-Able story, which he titled *East of Eden.*

In the Bible, Cain and Abel are brothers, the children of the first people, Adam and Eve. Both are farmers who give offerings to God. Cain's offering of produce does not please God as much as Abel's sacrifice of livestock. As a result, Cain becomes jealous of Abel and kills him. When God asks Cain where his brother is, the murderer replies, "Am I my brother's keeper?" God punishes Cain by condemning him to a lifetime of wandering from place to place.

George and Lennie are not brothers, but they display a

*A French engraving depicts the death of Abel at his brother's hand.*

brotherly concern for one another. Both work on farms, but throughout the story Lennie is associated with animals—a bear, a horse, mice, rabbits, puppies—making him a type of Abel figure. In the end of the book, he is slain by his Cain-like brother, George. The essence of Steinbeck's story is summed up in the question that Cain asks God, "Am I my brother's keeper?" In Steinbeck's version, the answer is yes. George cannot escape responsibility for his brother's well-being.

Unlike *East of Eden, Of Mice and Men* is not intended as a retelling of the biblical story. Instead, Steinbeck uses motifs from the story to deepen and enrich his tale of the migrant workers. "The implications of the Cain-and-Abel drama are everywhere apparent in the fable of George and Lennie and provide its mythic vehicle,"[100] writes scholar William Goldhurst. Anger and distrust are evident in both stories, as are the themes of temptation, sacrifice, and perpetual wandering.

The ranch that George and Lennie dream of owning resembles a paradise, a Garden of Eden. Goldhurst suggests that Steinbeck gave George the last name of Milton as a reference to John Milton, the author of the epic poem *Paradise Lost,* which tells the story of how Adam and Eve were cast out of the Garden of Eden. Scholar Peter Lisca points out that many of the characters in *Of Mice and Men* have names that begin with the first letter of Cain's name—Candy, Carlson, Crooks, Curley, and Curley's wife. Two other characters have the initials of Abel and Cain—Aunt Clara and Andy Cushman. The story is laced with curse words, including *God damn, Christ knows,* and *Jesus Christ,* that not only realistically depict how ranch hands speak but also seem to invoke God throughout the story. "Steinbeck's technique includes verbal ambiguity in place names and character names, *double entendre* [double meanings] in certain key passages of dialogue, and a mythical-allegorical drift that invites the reader into areas of philosophical and theological inquiry," writes Goldhurst. "On an allegorical level, *Of Mice and Men* reflects the early chapters of the Book of Genesis and the questions that grow out of the incidents therein depicted. These consist primarily of the consideration of man as a creature alone or as a brother and companion to others."[101]

## A Christian Parable

Steinbeck's "allegorical drift" is not confined to the story of Cain and Abel. Some scholars see Christian parallels in the story of Lennie and George. One simple example arises from the days covered in the story. George and Lennie eat their private meal on a Thursday night, arrive at the ranch on Friday, with the action culminating on a Sunday. These days correspond to the Christian Passion Week, beginning with Jesus' Passover meal with his disciples on Thursday, his crucifixion on Friday, and his resurrection on Sunday. According to Christian tradition, the death of Jesus is a sacrifice made to take away the Original Sin committed by Adam and Eve and to restore human beings to Paradise, not on the earth but in heaven. Critic Lee Dacus contends that the dream of the ranch with rabbits parallels the heavenly promise: "As with a traditional Christian, Lennie's hope and delight is not in the present, but in the glorious future."[102]

In Dacus's opinion, George ministers to Lennie much as Jesus ministered to his disciples. "George tells over again the promise of the farm, the pleasant evenings by the fire, and the endless and incomparable pleasures Lennie will enjoy feeding, tending, and playing with the (heavenly) rabbits."[103] Like Jesus, George tells Lennie to resist temptation and be good. He also issues warnings of what will happen if Lennie gives in to evil. George fulfills his Christ-like mission at the end of the book. He hears Lennie's confession and accepts it with love. He assures Lennie that he is not angry. He paints such a vivid picture of Paradise that Lennie begs him to leave for the ranch right away. With Lennie's eyes looking across the river, George dispatches his friend from the harsh and cruel world that is closing in on him. "Thus Lennie's perilous journey ends in the merciful hands of his guide and protector," writes Dacus. "The symbol of death is relegated to the ashheap of the past. And if the reader is impelled to feel that Lennie portrays the Christian figure, he is almost convinced that George, himself, has many of the attributes of the Christ he has been forced to impersonate."[104]

# Notes

## Introduction: Theater of the Mind

1. Mark Van Doren, "*Of Mice and Men* by John Steinbeck," *Nation*, March 6, 1937, p. 17.

2. Quoted in Susan Shillinglaw, introduction to *Of Mice and Men*, by John Steinbeck. New York: Penguin Books, 1994, pp. xv–xvi.

3. Otto Reinhart, *Drama, an Introductory Anthology*. Boston: Little, Brown, 1961, p. 90.

## Chapter One: The Life of John Steinbeck

4. Quoted in Jill Karson, ed., *Readings on "Of Mice and Men."* San Diego: Greenhaven, 1998, p. 14.

5. Quoted in Nelson Valjean, *John Steinbeck, the Errant Knight: An Intimate Biography of His California Years*. San Francisco: Chronicle Books, 1975, pp. 43–44.

6. Quoted in Karson, *Readings on "Of Mice and Men,"* p. 15.

7. Quoted in R.S. Hughes, *John Steinbeck: A Study of the Short Fiction*. Boston: Twayne, 1989, pp. 7–8.

8. Quoted in Jay Parini, *John Steinbeck: A Biography*. New York: Henry Holt, 1995, p. 27.

9. Quoted in Karson, *Readings on "Of Mice and Men,"* p. 18.

10. Quoted in Hughes, *John Steinbeck*, p. 6.

11. Quoted in Parini, *John Steinbeck*, p. 53.

12. John Steinbeck, "Autobiography: Making of a New Yorker," *New York Times Magazine*, February 1, 1953, p. 27.

13. Quoted in Parini, *John Steinbeck*, p. 99.

14. Quoted in Parini, *John Steinbeck*, p. 99.

15. Quoted in Karson, *Readings on "Of Mice and Men,"* p. 24.

16. John Steinbeck, introduction to *Short Novels of John Steinbeck*. New York: Viking, 1953, p. ii.

17. Steinbeck, introduction to *Short Novels of John Steinbeck*, p. iii.

18. Quoted in Karson, *Readings on "Of Mice and Men,"* pp. 26–27.

19. Quoted in Parini, *John Steinbeck,* p. 383.

20. Quoted in Warren French, *John Steinbeck,* Boston: Twayne, 1975, p. 34.

## Chapter 2: The Impact of the Novel

21. Quoted in Shillinglaw, introduction to *Of Mice and Men,* p. xix.

22. Quoted in Shillinglaw, introduction to *Of Mice and Men,* p. xxii.

23. Van Doren, "*Of Mice and Men* by John Steinbeck," p. 17.

24. Quoted in Shillinglaw, introduction to *Of Mice and Men,* p. xxiii.

25. Quoted in Shillinglaw, introduction to *Of Mice and Men,* p. xxiii.

26. Burton Rascoe, "John Steinbeck," *English Journal,* March 1938, p. 36.

27. Rascoe, "John Steinbeck," p. 38.

28. Quoted in Shillinglaw, introduction to *Of Mice and Men,* p. xxv.

29. Quoted in Shillinglaw, introduction to *Of Mice and Men,* p. xxiv.

30. Quoted in Shillinglaw, introduction to *Of Mice and Men,* p. xxiv.

31. Van Doren, "*Of Mice and Men* by John Steinbeck," p. 17.

32. Quoted in Shillinglaw, introduction to *Of Mice and Men,* p. xxiv.

33. Quoted in Shillinglaw, introduction to *Of Mice and Men,* p. xxv.

## Chapter 3: The Plot

34. Quoted in Shillinglaw, introduction to *Of Mice and Men,* pp. xv–xvi.

35. Steinbeck, *Of Mice and Men,* p. 6.

36. Steinbeck, *Of Mice and Men,* p. 13.

37. Steinbeck, *Of Mice and Men,* p. 15.

38. Steinbeck, *Of Mice and Men,* p. 20.

39. Steinbeck, *Of Mice and Men,* p. 22.

40. Steinbeck, *Of Mice and Men,* p. 23.

41. Steinbeck, *Of Mice and Men,* p. 27.

42. Steinbeck, *Of Mice and Men,* p. 32.

43. Steinbeck, *Of Mice and Men,* p. 34.

44. Steinbeck, *Of Mice and Men,* p. 59.

45. Steinbeck, *Of Mice and Men*, p. 61.

46. Steinbeck, *Of Mice and Men*, p. 72.

47. Steinbeck, *Of Mice and Men*, p. 71.

48. Steinbeck, *Of Mice and Men*, p. 78.

49. Steinbeck, *Of Mice and Men*, p. 79.

50. Steinbeck, *Of Mice and Men*, p. 81.

51. Steinbeck, *Of Mice and Men*, p. 84.

52. Steinbeck, *Of Mice and Men*, p. 85.

53. Steinbeck, *Of Mice and Men*, p. 89.

54. Steinbeck, *Of Mice and Men*, p. 92.

55. Steinbeck, *Of Mice and Men*, p. 94.

56. Steinbeck, *Of Mice and Men*, p. 100.

57. Steinbeck, *Of Mice and Men*, p. 103.

58. Steinbeck, *Of Mice and Men*, p. 105.

## Chapter 4: The Cast of Characters

59. Steinbeck, *Of Mice and Men*, p. 22.

60. Steinbeck, *Of Mice and Men*, p. 26.

61. Steinbeck, *Of Mice and Men*, p. 35.

62. Steinbeck, *Of Mice and Men*, p. 5.

63. Steinbeck, *Of Mice and Men*, p. 87.

64. Steinbeck, *Of Mice and Men*, p. 88.

65. Steinbeck, *Of Mice and Men*, p. 85.

66. Steinbeck, *Of Mice and Men*, p. 87.

67. Steinbeck, *Of Mice and Men*, p. 58.

68. Steinbeck, *Of Mice and Men*, p. 59.

69. Steinbeck, *Of Mice and Men*, p. 33.

70. Steinbeck, *Of Mice and Men*, p. 45.

71. Steinbeck, *Of Mice and Men*, p. 34.

72. Steinbeck, *Of Mice and Men*, p. 41.

73. Steinbeck, *Of Mice and Men*, p. 63.

74. Steinbeck, *Of Mice and Men,* p. 104.

75. Steinbeck, *Of Mice and Men,* p. 105.

76. Steinbeck, *Of Mice and Men,* p. 67.

77. Steinbeck, *Of Mice and Men,* p. 72.

78. Steinbeck, *Of Mice and Men,* p. 78.

79. Steinbeck, *Of Mice and Men,* p. 75.

80. Steinbeck, *Of Mice and Men,* p. 81.

81. Steinbeck, *Of Mice and Men,* p. 28.

82. Steinbeck, *Of Mice and Men,* p. 94.

83. Steinbeck, *Of Mice and Men,* p. 95.

84. Steinbeck, *Of Mice and Men,* p. 94.

## Chapter 5: Critical Analysis

85. B. Ramachandra Rao, *The American Fictional Hero.* New Delhi, India: Bahri Publications, 1979, p. 54.

86. Quoted in William S. Myers and Walter H. Newton, *The Hoover Administration: A Documented Narrative.* New York: Charles Scribner's Sons, 1936, pp. 63–64.

87. Quoted in Studs Terkel, *Hard Times: An Oral History of the Depression.* New York: Random House, 1970, pp. 450–451.

88. Quoted in William Dudley, ed., *The Great Depression: Opposing Viewpoints.* San Diego: Greenhaven, 1994, p. 45.

89. Steinbeck, *Of Mice and Men,* p. 15.

89. Steinbeck, *Of Mice and Men,* p. 71.

91. Quoted in Karson, *Readings on "Of Mice and Men,"* p. 53.

92. Steinbeck, introduction to *Short Novels of John Steinbeck,* p. ii.

93. Quoted in Shillinglaw, introduction to *Of Mice and Men,* pp. xx–xxi.

94. Steinbeck, *Of Mice and Men,* p. 77.

95. Steinbeck, *Of Mice and Men,* p. 33.

96. Steinbeck, *Of Mice and Men,* p. 95.

97. Steinbeck, *Of Mice and Men,* p. 53.

98. Van Doren, "*Of Mice and Men* by John Steinbeck," p. 17.

99. Leo Gurko, *"Of Mice and Men:* Steinbeck as Manichean," *University of Windsor Review,* vol. 8, no. 2, Spring 1973, p. 44.

100. William Goldhurst, *"Of Mice and Men:* John Steinbeck's Parable of the Curse of Cain," *Western American Review,* vol. 6, no. 2, Summer 1971, p. 127.

101. Goldhurst, *"Of Mice and Men,"* pp. 134–135.

102. Lee Dacus, "Lennie as Christian in *Of Mice and Men," Southwest American Literature,* vol. 4, 1974, p. 89.

103. Dacus, "Lennie as Christian in *Of Mice and Men,"* p. 89.

104. Dacus, "Lennie as Christian in *Of Mice and Men,"* p. 91.

# For Further Exploration

Below are some suggestions for potential essays on *Of Mice and Men*.

1. John Steinbeck's working title for *Of Mice and Men* was *Something That Happened*. At the suggestion of his friend Edward Ricketts, Steinbeck changed the title to incorporate a phrase from the Robert Burns poem "To a Mouse On Turning Her Up in Her Nest with a Plow." Discuss the two titles and how they influence your understanding of the work. *See also* Paul McCarthy, *John Steinbeck*; Richard Astro, *John Steinbeck and Edward F. Ricketts: The Shaping of a Novelist*; Joseph Fontenrose, *John Steinbeck: An Introduction and Interpretation; and* Louis Owens, *John Steinbeck's Re-Vision of America*.

2. In a tragedy, the main character strives to achieve something and fails, usually because of some inner trait or tragic flaw. In these strivings, the tragic hero often comes to some understanding that he or she lacked at the outset. Is *Of Mice and Men* a tragedy? If so, who is the tragic hero and why? What understanding is reached by the characters or the audience? *See also* Harry Thornton Moore, *The Novels of John Steinbeck*; Burton Rascoe, "John Steinbeck," *English Journal*, March 1938; Samuel I. Bellman, "Control and Freedom in Steinbeck's *Of Mice and Men*," *CEA Critic*, November 1975.

3. Lennie, George, and most of the other ranch hands are itinerant workers—that is, they do not have steady jobs but instead travel from ranch to ranch and do whatever work is available. Berry Burgum writes that Steinbeck's subject matter represents "a shift of attitude, general to the thirties, from the traditional absorption of American fiction with the problems and personages of the middle classes to an intense curiosity about the poor." Do you believe that Steinbeck's portrayal of impoverished workers is realistic? Why might he have chosen to depict people from a different economic class than his own? What does *Of Mice and Men* say about people from different classes? *See also* Berry Burgum, "The Sensibility of John Steinbeck," *Science and Society*, Spring 1946; B. Ramachandra Rao, *The American Fictional Hero*.

4. Steinbeck often compares Lennie to an animal. He writes that Lennie drinks like a horse and has hands that resemble paws. What other animals are associated with Lennie? How do these descriptions influence your attitude toward Lennie and your view of his actions toward Curley's wife? *See also* Peter Lisca, *The Wide World of John Steinbeck*.

5. When Steinbeck adapted *Of Mice and Men* for the stage, he cut the scene at the end of the book in which Lennie has visions of his Aunt Clara and a large, talking rabbit. Why do you think these scenes were cut? What purpose did they serve in the book? Would the book be better without them also? Why or why not? *See also* Howard Levant, *The Novels of John Steinbeck: A Critical Study.*

6. Many people believe that the themes of *Of Mice and Men* are too mature and its language is too vulgar to be required reading for children and young adults. Do you agree or disagree, and why? What age limit, if any, should be placed on reading this book? *See also* Richard Hoffstedt, "Steinbeck and Censorship," *Steinbeck Newsletter,* vol. 4, no. 1, Winter 1991.

7. Some critics see the conflicts in *Of Mice and Men* as a struggle between good and evil. Which characters are good, and which are evil? What is Steinbeck saying about the nature of evil? *See also* Samuel I. Bellman, "Control and Freedom in Steinbeck's *Of Mice and Men,*" *CEA Critic,* November 1975; Lee Dacus, "Lennie as Christian in *Of Mice and Men,*" *Southwest American Literature,* vol. 4, 1974; Leo Gurko, *"Of Mice and Men:* Steinbeck as Manichean," *University of Windsor Review,* vol. 8, no. 2, Spring 1973.

8. In a letter, John Steinbeck wrote that *Of Mice and Men* is "a study of the dreams and pleasures of everyone in the world." Lennie and George share a dream about owning a ranch together, and Candy and Crooks also become interested in the dream. In the end, however, the dream is destroyed. Who believes in the dream and why? Is the dream realistic? Why or why not? What is Steinbeck saying about the need for people to have a goal or a dream? *See also* Joseph Fontenrose, *John Steinbeck: An Introduction and Interpretation;* Susan Shillinglaw, introduction to *Of Mice and Men* (1994).

9. Steinbeck is often described as a lyrical writer, meaning that his prose has poetic qualities and creates a feeling of rapture. Do you believe that *Of Mice and Men* is a lyrical work? What sections do you feel are most lyrical? Why? Does lyricism contribute to or detract from the drama presented? *See also* R. Ganapathy, "Steinbeck's *Of Mice and Men:* A Study of Lyricism Through Primitivism," *Literary Criterion,* Winter 1962.

10. Steinbeck uses a great deal of foreshadowing in *Of Mice and Men* —that is, events occur early in the book that suggest what will happen later. For example, the shooting of Candy's dog in the third section foreshadows the shooting of Lennie in the last section. Give two other examples of foreshadowing. Some critics have

argued that Steinbeck uses foreshadowing too often in *Of Mice and Men*. Do you agree or disagree? Explain your answer by referring to the shooting of Candy's dog and the other two examples of foreshadowing that you have discussed. *See also* Howard Levant, *The Novels of John Steinbeck: A Critical Study;* Michael Shurgot, "A Game of Cards in Steinbeck's *Of Mice and Men,*" *Steinbeck Quarterly,* vol. 15, nos. 1–2, Winter/Spring 1982.

# Appendix of Criticism

## Our Animal Nature

The chief subject of Mr. Steinbeck's fiction has been not those aspects of humanity in which it is most thoughtful, imaginative, constructive, nor even those aspects of animals that seem most attractive to humans, but rather the processes of life itself. In the natural course of nature, living organisms are continually being destroyed, and among the principal things that destroy them are the predatory appetite and the competitive instinct that are necessary for the very survival of eating and breeding creatures. This impulse of the killer has been preserved in a simpleton like Lennie in a form in which it is almost innocent; and yet Lennie has learned from his more highly developed friend that to yield to it is to do something "bad." In his struggle against the instinct, he loses. Is Lennie bad or good? He is portrayed as, Mr. Steinbeck implies, all our human intentions are: by the uncertainties of our animal nature.

Edmund Wilson, *The Boys in the Back Room: Notes on California Novelists*. San Francisco: Colt, 1941.

## Hand Imagery

On one level [hand imagery] serves simply as an element of characterization. Thus Lennie's hands are more like "paws"; George has "small, strong hands"; Curley keeps one hand in a glove full of vaseline; Crooks has pink palms; Candy is missing a hand; the hands of Curley's wife are referred to only as fingers and red fingernails; Slim has large, capable hands "delicate in their action as those of a temple dancer." But this use of hand imagery falls far short of accounting for the well over one hundred times that it appears in this short novelette. Steinbeck sometimes seems to go out of the way for an excuse to use the word "hand," or insists on using the word when it is already implied, as in "He carried one small willow stick in his hand." Frequently, hands are seen as almost independent of the person himself: "His [Lennie's] hands went into the pocket again"; "Lennie's closed hand slowly obeyed"; "George . . . looked at his right hand that had thrown the gun away"; "Slim . . . looked down at his hands; he subdued one hand with the other and held it down."

Curiously, the common use of the word "hand" to mean simply a workman, especially on farms and ranches, occurs only once. But perhaps this is the root source of all the hand images. The lives of the characters are so circumscribed that they are more hands than complete men. Curley is said to be "handy," but Lennie "ain't handy." Yet the incident in which Curley attacks Lennie is clearly described in terms of hands; and, symbolically, it concludes with Curley's hand being crushed in the huge paws of Lennie.

Peter Lisca, *John Steinbeck: Nature and Myth.*
New York: Cromwell, 1978.

## A Knight of the Round Table

Although other critics have not noted to what extent *Of Mice and Men* is an Arthurian story, the fundamental parallels—the knightly loyalty, the pursuit of the vision, the creation of a bond (shared briefly by Candy and Crooks), and its destruction by an at least potentially adulterous relationship—are there. They are, however, so concealed by the surface realism of the work that one unfamiliar with Steinbeck's previous Arthurian experiments would be hardly likely to notice them. The one obvious Arthurian hangover is George, who is not only remarkably loyal to his charge—the feeble-minded Lennie—but also remarkably pure.

George not only warns Lennie against the blandishments of Curley's wife, but is himself obviously impervious to her charms. While the other ranch hands are excited by her presence, George says only, "Jesus, what a tramp!" When invited to join the boys in a Saturday night trip to a neighboring town's "nice" whorehouse, George says that he "might go in an' set and have a shot," but "ain't puttin' out no two and a half." He excuses himself on the ground that he is saving money to buy a farm, but not even Galahad might have found it politic to profess chastity in a bunkhouse. George seems to have stepped, in fact, not out of [British writer Sir Thomas] Malory's Arthurian stories but [British writer Alfred Lord] Tennyson's. When he is told that Curley boasts of having his glove full of Vaseline in order to keep his hand soft for his wife, George says, "That's a dirty thing to tell around."

George is noticeably more critical of Curley's wife than Steinbeck is. *Of Mice and Men* is not so completely objective as *In Dubious Battle;* Steinbeck editorializes occasionally, for example after the girl has been killed:

> . . . the meanness and the plannings and the discontent and the ache for attention were all gone from her face. She was very pretty and simple and her face was sweet and young.

George shows no such sympathy, and it is important to notice that the author is more flexible than his character, because it is a sign that he is not being carried away by his vision as are the characters sometimes assumed to represent his viewpoint. Like Jim Nolan [in *In Dubious Battle*], George is a last Galahad, dismounted, armed only with a fading dream, a long way from Camelot. Steinbeck is his historian, not his alter ego.

Warren French, *John Steinbeck*.
Boston: Twayne, 1975.

## A Game of Cards as a Symbol

Midway through section two of *Of Mice and Men* . . . Steinbeck describes George walking to the table in the bunkhouse and shuffling some of the playing cards lying there. Often during the rest of section two and throughout section three, Steinbeck pictures George playing solitaire with these cards. Although George's card-playing may seem just a means of passing time during his and Lennie's first night on the ranch, the frequency of George's card games and Steinbeck's careful juxtaposition of them with the prophetic events of sections two and three indicate that the game of cards is the central symbol of the entire novel. . . .

Lester Jay Marks writes that Steinbeck's novel is "disciplined by his non-teleological methods of observing 'phenomena.' He is concerned not with the why but with the *what* and *how* of the individual's illusions." Steinbeck's original title, "Something That Happened," is, according to Marks, an unsentimental comment upon the "tragic reversal of fortunes" that George and Lennie experience. A non-teleological world is one of chance, of reversals of fortune beyond man's comprehension or his power to control. And a game of cards is an exact symbol of this kind of world. In card games there is no pattern to the cards' random appearance; their sequence is solely a matter of chance. Analogically, although George tries to control Lennie's activities and movements on the ranch, he cannot prevent Lennie's tragic meeting with Curley's wife in the barn. . . .

Steinbeck enhances the general symbolism of George's games of solitaire by carefully interweaving them into the narrative of sections two and three. George first plays with the cards during his conversation with Candy about Curley and his wife. . . . George's card games precede and follow the appearance of Curley's wife and Lennie's reactions to her, thus symbolically framing their first meeting in the realm of chance. Further, when Slim enters he sits down at the table across from George. While Slim plays with the cards, he talks to Carlson about his dog's pups and Candy's old dog. This conversation foreshadows Lennie's death; and the sense of his and the dog's similar fates is suggested by the hand of cards that George and Slim, with ironic nonchalance, manipulate during this scene. . . .

Section three opens with George's confiding in Slim about Lennie's troubles in Weed. Twice during their dialogue Steinbeck describes

George playing solitaire. . . . Steinbeck's careful interweaving of George's hand of solitaire with his narrative of Lennie's seizure of the girl in Weed is his most effective apposition in the novel. Lennie's actions in Weed clearly presage his killing of Curley's wife, and George will be alone after he shoots Lennie. . . .

In the final moments of section three, Steinbeck's disciplined non-teleological vision is clearly evident; chance rules in the bunkhouse as later it will in the barn. The genius of Steinbeck's narrative in *Of Mice and Men* lies in the consistency of this vision, and in George's card games Steinbeck provides an exact symbol of the unpredictable, often merciless world in which his characters vainly strive to maintain their dignity and fulfill their dreams.

> Michael Shurgot, "A Game of Cards in Steinbeck's
> *Of Mice and Men,*" *Steinbeck Quarterly,* vol. 15,
> nos. 1–2, Winter/Spring 1982.

## A Parable of the Human Condition

*Of Mice and Men* was meant to be a non-teleological tale and the first title that Steinbeck gave it was "Something That Happened." Something that happens may be accidental, coincidental, atypical, and surely the concluding events and deeds in this novel are neither typical nor commonplace. For George and Lennie, being who they are and where they are, the outcome may be inevitable, and we may see a personal tragedy in the tale. Steinbeck, however, meant the story to be a parable of the human condition, as his final title indicates. It is a good title, because the story itself tells us just what [poet Robert] Burns meant when he said, "the best-laid schemes o' mice an' men gang aft agley" one unlucky fieldmouse lost its nest when the field was plowed. But not all fieldmice suffer that fate; Burns did not mean that no man's scheme is ever realized. Steinbeck reads, "All schemes o' mice an' men gang ever agley." Crooks said, "Nobody never gets to heaven, and nobody gets no land," and George said to Candy, "—I think I knowed from the very first. I think I knowed we'd never do her," thus reading destiny—the inevitable failure of his plans—in Lennie's terrible deed. It is the message of *Cup of Gold,* the vanity of human wishes. In a letter to his agents, written soon after completing the manuscript of *Of Mice and Men,* Steinbeck said that Lennie represents "the inarticulate and powerful yearning of all men," and referred to its scene as a microcosm, making it plain that the novel was meant to express the inevitable defeat and futility of all men's plans. But the tragic story of George and Lennie cannot carry the load of cosmic pessimism placed upon it. It tells us only that it is hard for bindlestiffs to buy land, and that even when they get the money they cannot be sure of making the purchase. Nevertheless, migratory workers have acquired land, even in California, and George could have done so. Not Lennie who died, but Candy who lived, had $350, and Candy still wanted to carry out the plan. Objectively considered, the prospects for success were better without Lennie, who would surely have killed every rabbit on the place. But without Lennie the plan had no meaning for George. The sweeping pessimistic thesis is thus imposed upon the story and obscures its true meaning: that our pleasures often oppose and thwart our schemes. Steinbeck came nearer to an adequate statement of thesis when he said in another letter that *Of Mice and Men* was "a study of the dreams and pleasures of everyone in the world."

> Joseph Fontenrose, *John Steinbeck: An Introduction and Interpretation*. New York: Barnes and Noble, 1963.

## Christian Symbolism in *Of Mice and Men*

Perhaps the greatest appeal of John Steinbeck's Lennie in *Of Mice and Men* comes from the fact that his character is cast as the traditional Christian figure worthy of the pen of [seventeenth-century English preacher and writer John] Bunyan. The echoes of this parallel, however, touch the reader as subtle overtones. And this writer admits to having read the novel more than once before this aspect of the author's meaning became apparent.

In this study of Lennie it is seen that, pure in heart but burdened with his great hulk of flesh to carry, he lumbers through life during the Great Depression crushing and killing, without intent, the things which please him or that he loves. Dreaming of his own special heaven, and trying to be obedient but unable to attain this, he, nevertheless, maintains his faith in his lord and master. In the final chapter, he dies looking across the river of his rendezvous with death (and George), unafraid, his dream of paradise before him.

If, then, Lennie serves as the Christian figure, we are forced to conclude that George, in the role of Lennie's only friend, his source of protection, aid, faith, and finally the instrument of his death, must stand, though much less well-defined, as the Christ figure. . . .

As the story opens, the reader finds the two friends walking wearily along a lonely, dusty road. In this scene George is verbally chastising Lennie for his transgressions. Lennie has stumbled into trouble in the town of Weed, and George has rescued him from an angry mob by hiding with him in the water of an irrigation ditch until they can make their escape in the night. This appears at second glance to mirror the ritual of baptism. In the present scene, however, Lennie is pained by the displeasure of George and asks for forgiveness, pleading to be told about the paradisical farm where George has promised that they will live (forever) and raise rabbits.

As they walk along, George discovers that Lennie is fondling a dead mouse which he is carrying in his jumper pocket. This may well represent the residue of dead sin which Christian yet carries about his person after regeneration; for his pleasure in stroking the mouse is exactly the same type of sin which almost lost him his life back in Weed. Lennie is punished and purified: George makes him reluctantly throw away the dead mouse and go in search of firewood. He brings back a few puny twigs and also, furtively, the carcass of the mouse. This entire scene very effectively illustrates the penitence of the Christian and the tendency of the flesh to return to the mortality of sin and death. The small quantity of firewood brought in by Lennie may also point up the inconsequentiality of Christian's works.

Lennie is again deprived of the mouse as George reads the guilt written on his face. Thus, the mouse becomes a complex symbol and foreshadowing device, signifying, at least, pleasure, sin, and death. But in addition to this, it constitutes a symbolic object in an important parallel: Even as the mouse's death is at the unintentional hands of Lennie who cared for it and wished it no ill, the death of Lennie is likewise at the hands of George who cared greatly for him and wished him only the best.

After George's exasperation has subsided, the two are preparing their supper on the river bank. . . . This scene is prayer-like in essence. The kneeling Lennie looks into the darkness of death across a river that seems ominous and offers to leave his friend if that is his will. The reply comes in the form of an impatient question: "Where the hell would you go?" This suggests that anywhere Lennie goes without George will be hell. The expletive George utters seems to be more significant than mere habit of speech: "*Jesus Christ,* somebody'd shoot you for a coyote." This is also an instance of sharp dramatic irony since it will be George who will do the shooting at last. "No, you stay with me," is uttered in the kindly tones of one who cares.

A little later, having forgotten George's impatience, Lennie begs to be told the story of the little farm they dream of. . . . As with the traditional Christian, Lennie's hope and delight is not in the present, but in the glorious future. George tells over again the promise of the farm, the pleasant evenings by the fire, and the endless and incomparable pleasures Lennie will enjoy feeding, tending, and playing with the (heavenly) rabbits. . . .

Later at the ranch, except for the fight with Curley, which might well symbolize Christian's struggle with Satan, Lennie mainly stays clear of trouble through the watchful protection of George, until the fatal scene in the barn out of George's sight in which Lennie kills the girl. This is through no intent but merely a product of childlike excitability and tremendous physical strength. Sensing that he is in deep trouble, Lennie makes his way to the spot along the river bank where he had promised to hide and wait for George.

George, realizing that Lennie's time is up, that he is about to be lynched by the enraged men, now takes the ugly-looking Luger (death) and goes sadly to find his friend with the huge and deadly body coupled with the tiny and innocent mind. He finds Lennie sitting hidden in the brush as the sounds of the manhunters come nearer. . . .

Finally, George can wait no longer. The posse is near. He tells the transported Lennie of the beautiful future, the farm and the rabbits, and the love, where people will give a "hoot in hell" about each other. He assures Lennie that he is not "mad.". . .

Thus Lennie's perilous journey ends in the merciful hands of his guide and protector, who feels at the moment that this essential deed of love is an act of betrayal. The symbol of death is relegated to the ashheap of the past. And if the reader is impelled to feel that Lennie portrays the Christian figure, he is almost convinced that George, himself, has many of the attributes of the Christ he has been forced to impersonate.

Lee Dacus, "Lennie as Christian in Of Mice and Men,"<br>Southwest American Literature, vol. 4, 1974.

## The Play Format Limits the Development of the Story

It would seem that [*Of Mice and Men*] was intended to function as a play, and Steinbeck did not alter the novel in any essential during the tinkering in preparation for the New York stage production. . . . And clearly the novel does "play": Characters make entrances and exits; plainly indicated parallels and oppositions that are characteristic of the drama exist in quantity and function as they should; suspense is maintained; characters are kept uncomplicated and "active" in the manner of stage characterization; since there is little internal or implicit development, events depend on what is said or done in full view; the locale is restricted mainly to one place; the span of time is brief; the central theme is stated and restated—the good life is impossible because humanity is flawed—and in itself is deeply poignant, as Steinbeck had defined a play-novelette theme. In short, I do not see how *Of Mice and Men* could meet more completely the specifications of a play-novelette as Steinbeck listed them. If critics have been displeased with *Of Mice and Men,* as Steinbeck was, the trouble cannot lie in the application of the theory but in the assumption that inspired the theory. . . . As a dramatic structure, *Of Mice and Men* is focused on Lennie and occurs within the context of the bunkhouse and the ranch. Within these confines, Steinbeck develops theme and countertheme by exploring the chances for the good life against the flawed human material that Lennie symbolizes most completely and the code of rough justice that most people accept. Even this initial, limited statement points to the central difficulty in the novel. The "well-made" dramatic form that Steinbeck . . . did construct in *Of Mice and Men* is conducive to abstraction because it is limited to visible action. Lennie is limited in much the same way. As a huge, powerful semi-idiot who kills when he is frightened or simply when he is thoughtless, Lennie is a reduction of humanity to the lowest common denominator. It may be possible to construct a parable out of so limited a structure and materials, but it is impossible to handle complex human motives and relationships within those limits. *Of Mice and Men* is successful to the extent that it remains a parable, but the enveloping action is more complex than the parable form can encompass. . . .

A novel cannot be structured solely on the basis of a theme, even a fundamental theme. Too much else must be simplified. Worse, the unconventional morality located in friendship produces Lennie's death, not only because Steinbeck can see no other way to conclude. Lennie dies necessarily because friendship can go no further than it does go, and nothing can be made of the dreamlike ideal of the little farm. The extreme simplification is that Steinbeck can do nothing with Lennie after he has been exhibited. . . . Lennie must be killed off when his existence raises problems of characterization more complex than the play-novelette form can express. Materials and structure pull against each other and finally collapse into an oversimplified conclusion that removes rather than faces the central theme.

Howard Levant, *The Novels of John Steinbeck: A Critical Study.* Columbia: University of Missouri Press, 1974.

# Chronology

**1902**
John Steinbeck is born on February 27.

**1909**
Steinbeck's sister Mary is born.

**1914**
Steinbeck receives the pony, Jill, as a gift.

**1915**
Steinbeck enrolls in Salinas High School.

**1919**
Steinbeck graduates from Salinas High School and enters Stanford University.

**1920**
Steinbeck works on the Spreckels Sugar Company farm and gathers impressions about farm life.

**1925**
Steinbeck moves to New York, working as a laborer and as a reporter for the *American* newspaper.

**1926**
Steinbeck returns to California and resumes work on his stories and novel.

**1927**
The *Smoker's Companion* publishes Steinbeck's short story "The Gifts of Iban" in its March issue.

**1929**
Robert M. McBride and Company publishes Steinbeck's first novel, *Cup of Gold*.

**1930**
Steinbeck marries Carol Henning on January 14; he meets Edward Ricketts in Pacific Grove, California, that same year.

**1932**
Steinbeck publishes *Pastures of Heaven*.

# 1933
"The Red Pony" (retitled "The Gift") and "The Great Mountains" are published in *North American Review;* Steinbeck publishes *To a God Unknown.*

# 1934
Steinbeck wins the O. Henry Prize for "The Murder"; his mother dies.

# 1935
Pascal Covici becomes Steinbeck's publisher; Steinbeck publishes *Tortilla Flat,* "The White Quail," and "The Snake"; he receives the Commonwealth Club of California Gold Medal.

# 1936
Steinbeck publishes articles on migrants in the *San Francisco News,* as well as *In Dubious Battle,* "The Leader of the People," "The Vigilante," "Breakfast," and "Saint Katy the Virgin"; his father dies.

# 1937
Steinbeck publishes *The Red Pony* (first three parts), "Johnny Bear," "The Chrysanthemums," and *Of Mice and Men;* the Theater Union in San Francisco performs *Of Mice and Men* from the book; the stage version is performed on Broadway and wins the Drama Critics Circle Award.

# 1938
Steinbeck publishes *The Long Valley* and *Their Blood Is Strong,* a pamphlet based on *Sun* articles about migrants; he wins the O. Henry Prize for "The Promise."

# 1939
World War II begins in Europe; Steinbeck publishes *The Grapes of Wrath;* he is elected to the National Institute of Arts and Letters.

# 1940
Steinbeck and Ricketts take a research trip to the Sea of Cortez; Steinbeck wins the Pulitzer Prize for *The Grapes of Wrath;* he films *The Forgotten Village* in Mexico; the film versions of *The Grapes of Wrath* and *Of Mice and Men* are released.

# 1941
Japan bombs Pearl Harbor; America enters World War II; Steinbeck publishes *Sea of Cortez* with Ricketts.

## 1942

Steinbeck publishes *The Moon Is Down;* he writes the script for *Bombs Away;* he wins the O. Henry Prize for "How Edith McGillcuddy Met R.L.S."; Steinbeck and Carol Henning divorce; the film version of *Tortilla Flat* is released.

## 1943

Steinbeck marries Gwendolyn Conger; they move to New York; the film version of *The Moon is Down* is released.

## 1944

Steinbeck writes the script for *Lifeboat* with Alfred Hitchcock; his son Thom is born on August 2.

## 1945

World War II ends; Steinbeck publishes *Cannery Row; The Red Pony* is republished in four parts; "The Pearl of the World" appears in *Woman's Home Companion.*

## 1946

His son John is born on June 10.

## 1947

Steinbeck publishes "The Time the Wolves Ate the Vice-Principal," *The Wayward Bus,* and *The Pearl.*

## 1948

Steinbeck publishes "Miracle of Tepaya" and *A Russian Journal;* he is elected to American Academy of Letters; the film version of *The Pearl* is released; Edward Ricketts dies in an automobile accident; Steinbeck and Gwendolyn Conger divorce.

## 1949

The film version of *The Red Pony* is released; Steinbeck publishes "His Father."

## 1950

Steinbeck publishes *Burning Bright,* a novel and a play; he writes the script for *Viva Zapata!;* he marries Elaine Scott.

## 1951

Steinbeck publishes *The Log from "The Sea of Cortez."*

## 1952

Steinbeck publishes *East of Eden.*

## 1954
Steinbeck publishes *Sweet Thursday.*

## 1955
John and Elaine Steinbeck buy a house in Sag Harbor; the film version of *East of Eden* is released; he publishes "The Summer Before," "Affair at 7, Rue de M——," and "We're Holding Our Own" (retitled "The Short Story of Mankind").

## 1956
"Affair at 7, Rue de M——" wins Steinbeck's fourth and last O. Henry Prize.

## 1957
Steinbeck publishes "Case of the Hotel Ghost . . ." and *The Short Reign of Pippin IV, a Fabrication;* the film version of *The Wayward Bus* is released.

## 1958
Steinbeck publishes *Once There Was a War.*

## 1960
Steinbeck tours the United States with his dog, Charley.

## 1961
John F. Kennedy becomes president; Kennedy invites Steinbeck to his inauguration; Steinbeck publishes *The Winter of Our Discontent;* the film *Flight* released.

## 1962
Steinbeck publishes *Travels with Charley in Search of America;* he receives the Nobel Prize for literature.

## 1963
Steinbeck tours Europe for U.S. Cultural Exchange program; John F. Kennedy is assassinated; Lyndon Johnson becomes president.

## 1964–1975
The United States is involved in the Vietnam War.

## 1964
Steinbeck receives the U.S. Medal of Freedom.

## 1965
Steinbeck reports from Vietnam for *Newsday.*

## 1966
Steinbeck publishes *America and Americans.*

## 1968
The televised versions of *Travels with Charley, Of Mice and Men,* and *The Grapes of Wrath* air; Steinbeck dies on December 20; he is buried in Salinas.

## 1969
*Journal of a Novel: The "East of Eden" Letters* is published.

## 1970
The opera version of *Of Mice and Men* premiers.

## 1975
*Steinbeck: A Life in Letters,* edited by Elaine Steinbeck and Robert Wallstein, is published; *The Acts of King Arthur and His Noble Knights* is published.

## 1981
New televised version of *Of Mice and Men* airs.

## 1992
The new film version of *Of Mice and Men* is released.

# Works Consulted

## Major Editions of *Of Mice and Men*

John Steinbeck, *Of Mice and Men*. New York: Covici, Friede, 1937.

——, *Of Mice and Men*. New York: Penguin USA, 1993.

——, *Of Mice and Men*. Introduction by Susan Shillinglaw. New York: Penguin Books, 1994.

——, *Novels and Stories, 1932–1937: The Pastures of Heaven / To a God Unknown / Tortilla Flat / In Dubious Battle / Of Mice and Men*. New York: Library of America, 1994.

## Also by John Steinbeck

John Steinbeck, *The Acts of King Arthur and His Noble Knights*. Ed. Chase Horton. London: Heinemann, 1976. Steinbeck's unfinished translation from the Winchester manuscripts of Sir Thomas Malory and other sources.

——, *America and Americans*. New York: Viking, 1966. Steinbeck's reflections on his country and its citizens.

——, *Bombs Away: The Story of a Bomber Team*. New York: Viking, 1942. Suggested by General "Hap" Arnold of the U.S. Air Force, the book describes the training of bombardiers.

——, *Burning Bright*. New York: Viking, 1950. The story of a childless couple, Joe and Mordeen Saul, and the troubles they face when Mordeen becomes pregnant by another man.

——, *Cannery Row*. New York: Viking, 1945. An account of the adventures and misadventures of workers in a California cannery and their friends.

——, *Cup of Gold*. New York: Robert M. McBride, 1929. A fictionalized biography of English buccaneer Sir Henry Morgan.

——, *East of Eden*. New York: Viking, 1952. The story of two boys —one good and one bad—and their relationship with their stern father.

——, *The Forgotten Village*. New York: Viking, 1940. The screenplay for a motion picture about a Mexican village.

——, *The Grapes of Wrath*. New York: Viking, 1939. The story of an Oklahoma farm family, the Joads, who are driven off their homestead during the Great Depression and travel west to California.

————, *In Dubious Battle.* New York: Covici, Friede, 1936. Set in California apple country, the novel depicts the workers' bitter revolt against the landowners and working conditions.

————, *Journal of a Novel: The "East of Eden" Letters.* New York: Viking, 1969. Notes made by Steinbeck about the composition of *East of Eden.*

————, *The Log from "The Sea of Cortez."* New York: Viking, 1951. A version of the log Steinbeck kept during his specimen-gathering trip with Edward Ricketts in the Gulf of California.

————, *The Long Valley.* New York: Viking, 1938. Fifteen short stories, most of which are set in the Salinas Valley or the coastal mountains nearby.

————, *The Moon Is Down.* New York: Viking, 1942. Steinbeck explores the effects of the Nazi invasion on a small town in Norway during World War II.

————, *The Moon Is Down.* New York: Viking, 1943. The stage version of Steinbeck's World War II novel.

————, *Of Mice and Men.* New York: Covici, Friede, 1937. The stage adaptation of the popular novel.

————, *Once There Was a War.* New York: Viking, 1958. A collection of Steinbeck's war dispatches, with an introduction by the author.

————, *The Pastures of Heaven.* New York: Brewer, Warren & Putnam, 1932. A collection of stories about the arrival of a family, the Munroes, to Corral de Tierra valley and the problems they cause.

————, *The Pearl.* New York: Viking, 1947. The story of a poor fisherman in La Paz, Mexico, who finds a large pearl "as perfect as the moon."

————, *The Red Pony.* 3 parts. New York: Covici, Friede, 1937. A series of three related short stories about a boy named Jody who raises a pony.

————, *The Red Pony.* 4 parts. New York: Viking, 1945. Four related short stories about a boy named Jody who lives on a ranch in Monterey County.

————, *A Russian Journal.* New York: Viking, 1948. A collaboration between Steinbeck and photographer Robert Capa, who traveled in Russia after World War II.

————, *The Short Reign of Pippin IV.* An allegory of the French political scene in the 1950s, this book tells the story of an astronomer turned king, who attempts to reform his nation.

————, *Sweet Thursday.* New York: Viking, 1954. A sequel to *Cannery Row*, this novel revives the characters of Doc, Mack, and others.

————, *Their Blood Is Strong.* San Francisco: Simon J. Lubin Society of California, 1938. Newspaper reports made to the *San Francisco News* in 1936 about migrant workers, with a conclusion by the author.

————, *To a God Unknown.* New York: Robert O. Ballou, 1933. New England families settle in the Salinas Valley and prosper until human failings and drought drive them away.

————, *Tortilla Flat.* New York: Covici, Friede, 1935. The exploits of a gang of *paisanos,* or poor Mexicans, who live in a shabby district of Monterey called Tortilla Flat.

————, *Travels with Charley in Search of America.* New York: Viking, 1962. Steinbeck's account of his journey across America with his poodle, Charley.

————, *Viva Zapata!* New York: Viking, 1974. This script of the 1952 film tells the story of Emiliano Zapata, who championed the cause of the peasants during the Mexican Revolution.

————, *The Wayward Bus.* New York: Viking, 1947. This novel presents a kind of modern-day morality play that is acted out among the passengers of a bus.

————, *The Winter of Our Discontent.* New York: Viking, 1961. A novel that takes a satirical look at Americans and their values in 1960.

John Steinbeck, with Edward F. Ricketts, *Sea of Cortez.* New York: Viking, 1941. An account of the 1940 trip to the Gulf of California that Steinbeck took with his biologist friend, Edward Ricketts.

## Film Adaptations

*The Grapes of Wrath* (1940)

*Of Mice and Men* (1940, 1992)

*The Moon Is Down* (1943)

*Lifeboat* (1944)

*The Pearl* (1948)

*The Red Pony* (1949)

*East of Eden* (1955)

*The Wayward Bus* (1957)

## Biographies of John Steinbeck

Richard Astro, *John Steinbeck and Edward F. Ricketts: The Shaping of a Novelist*. Minneapolis: University of Minnesota Press, 1973. A look at the impact of Ricketts's scientific beliefs on Steinbeck's approach to fiction.

Jackson J. Benson, *Looking for Steinbeck's Ghost*. Norman: University of Oklahoma Press, 1988. Describing the efforts that went into the writing of his definitive biography of Steinbeck, Benson explores "the relationship between art in the literary form, and man's mortality," concluding that Steinbeck "lives every day through the millions of words he left behind, and in the millions of eyes and minds which see and ponder his lifetime achievement of literary legacy."

————, *The True Adventures of John Steinbeck, Writer*. New York: Viking, 1984. In this massive one-thousand-page work, Benson draws on Steinbeck's papers, photographs, and interviews to explore every aspect of Steinbeck's life—his boyhood, his literary success, his marriages, and his relationship with his critics.

John Ditsky, *John Steinbeck: Life, Work, and Criticism*. Fredericton, New Brunswick, Canada: York, 1985. An overview of Steinbeck's life, with special attention to the reception of his work by the critical community.

Thomas Fensch, *Steinbeck and Covici: The Story of a Friendship*. Middlebury, VT: Paul S. Ericksson, 1979. An account of the lifelong friendship between Steinbeck and the man who published his works at his own firm and later at Viking Press.

Tom Ito, *The Importance of John Steinbeck*. San Diego: Lucent Books, 1994. This book discusses Steinbeck and his works in the context of the places he lived and the historical events that influenced his work.

Thomas Kiernan, *The Intricate Music: A Biography of John Steinbeck*. Boston: Little, Brown, 1979. Kiernan traces the evolution of Steinbeck's art and gives a picture of Steinbeck's fears, loves, and failures.

Paul McCarthy, *John Steinbeck*. New York: Frederick Ungar, 1980. The first major study of Steinbeck's life and work to appear after the author's death in 1968, this book focuses on Steinbeck's development of unique metaphors and symbolism. Chapter 3 discusses *Of Mice and Men* as an example of "Steinbeck's craftsmanship . . . at its best."

Elizabeth Meehan, *Twentieth Century American Authors*. San Diego: Lucent Books, 2000. Includes brief biographies of major American authors, including John Steinbeck, with an introductory essay on the evolution of American literature in the context of a rapidly changing society.

Jay Parini, *John Steinbeck: A Biography*. New York: Henry Holt, 1995. Drawing on interviews with dozens of people who knew Steinbeck intimately—including his beloved third wife, Elaine—as well as on published and unpublished letters, diaries, and manuscripts, Parini creates a sympathetic but revealing account of Steinbeck's life and relationships.

Elaine Steinbeck and Robert Wallsten, *Steinbeck: A Life in Letters*. New York: Viking, 1975. An extensive collection of Steinbeck's correspondence, assembled with the help and insight of his widow.

John Steinbeck, "Autobiography: Making of a New Yorker," *New York Times Magazine*, February 1, 1953. The author's reflections on how he came to reside in New York for most of the second half of his life.

Nelson Valjean, *John Steinbeck, the Errant Knight: An Intimate Biography of His California Years*. San Francisco: Chronicle Books, 1975. A meticulously researched account of the first half of Steinbeck's life.

## Literary Criticism

Samuel I. Bellman, "Control and Freedom in Steinbeck's *Of Mice and Men*," *CEA Critic*, vol. 38, no. 1, November 1975. In this essay, Bellman shows how George's efforts to control Lennie ended up placing controls on his own life.

Berry Burgum, "The Sensibility of John Steinbeck," *Science and Society*, Spring 1946. An exploration of Steinbeck's attitudes toward the poor.

Lee Dacus, "Lennie as Christian in *Of Mice and Men*," *Southwest American Literature*, vol. 4, 1974. This essay compares Lennie to John Bunyan's Christian and discusses other elements of Christianity in *Of Mice and Men*.

Joseph Fontenrose, *John Steinbeck: An Introduction and Interpretation.* New York: Barnes and Noble, 1963. A noted scholar of Greek and Roman literature describes the mythological component of Steinbeck's works.

Warren French, *John Steinbeck.* Boston: Twayne, 1975. A critical examination of Steinbeck's fiction, beginning with overview chapters and then proceeding through the works in chronological order. Chapter 5 discusses *Of Mice and Men* along with *In Dubious Battle* and *The Long Valley* as part of Steinbeck's movement from naturalism toward theater.

R. Ganapathy, "Steinbeck's *Of Mice and Men:* A Study of Lyricism Through Primitivism," *Literary Criterion,* vol. 5, no. 3, Winter 1962. This essay describes *Of Mice and Men* as a nostalgic, pastoral fantasy that achieves its lyric effect through prose that is highly charged with imagery and poetry.

William Goldhurst, "*Of Mice and Men:* John Steinbeck's Parable of the Curse of Cain," *Western American Review,* vol. 6, no. 2, Summer 1971. The author describes *Of Mice and Men* as a parable that echoes the biblical story of the brothers Cain and Abel.

Leo Gurko, "*Of Mice and Men:* Steinbeck as Manichean," *University of Windsor Review,* vol. 8, no. 2, Spring 1973. A reading of *Of Mice and Men* that draws on the ancient Manichean religion's tenets of an ongoing struggle (and balance between) good and evil.

Charlotte Cook Hadella, *"Mice and Men": A Kinship of Powerlessness.* New York: Twayne, 1995. A look at the forces that shaped the special bond between the characters in *Of Mice and Men.*

Tetsumaro Hayashi, ed., *A Study Guide to John Steinbeck: A Handbook to His Major Works.* Metuchen, NJ: Scarecrow, 1974. A selection of essays, each by a different author, analyzing Steinbeck's major works.

Richard Hoffstedt, "Steinbeck and Censorship," *Steinbeck Newsletter,* vol. 4, no. 1, Winter 1991. A brief discussion of various attempts to remove Steinbeck's works from schools and libraries.

R.S. Hughes, *John Steinbeck: A Study of the Short Fiction.* Boston: Twayne, 1989. An examination of the more than fifty short stories that make up Steinbeck's canon. In addition to his own analysis, Hughes offers selected writings by other critics as well as Steinbeck's own observations about short-story writing.

Jill Karson, ed., *Readings on "Of Mice and Men."* San Diego: Greenhaven, 1998. This book provides a brief overview of Steinbeck's life followed by essays by noted scholars on a wide range of themes, symbolism, and techniques in *Of Mice and Men.*

Howard Levant, *The Novels of John Steinbeck: A Critical Study.* Columbia: University of Missouri Press, 1974. A study of Steinbeck's use of dramatic and panoramic techniques to convey his philosophical beliefs in his fiction.

Peter Lisca, *John Steinbeck: Nature and Myth.* New York: Cromwell, 1978. A survey of Steinbeck's life, achievements, and work, with special emphasis on his treatment of nature and mythology.

———, *The Wide World of John Steinbeck.* New Brunswick, NJ: Rutgers University Press, 1958. A comprehensive study of Steinbeck's fiction that includes previously unpublished correspondence between Steinbeck and his agents and publishers.

Lester J. Marks, *Thematic Design in the Novels of John Steinbeck.* The Hague, Netherlands: Mouton, 1969. An examination of three recurring themes in Steinbeck's fiction: the human need for a god, the notion of human beings as "group animals," and the nonteleological focus on the process of life rather than on its ends.

Harry Thornton Moore, *The Novels of John Steinbeck.* Chicago: Normandie House, 1939. Subtitled "A First Critical Study," the book offers readers—especially those in Great Britain, where a shorter edition appeared—a look at Steinbeck's life and the land about which he wrote as well as contemporary criticism of the works.

Louis Owens, *John Steinbeck's Re-Vision of America.* Athens: University of Georgia Press, 1985. An analysis of major themes in Steinbeck's fiction.

B. Ramachandra Rao, *The American Fictional Hero.* New Delhi, India: Bahri Publications, 1979. A discussion of the traits of American literary heroes.

Burton Rascoe, "John Steinbeck," *English Journal,* March 1938. A review of the stage version of *Of Mice and Men* that hails the play as "an aesthetic miracle."

Otto Reinhart, *Drama, an Introductory Anthology.* Boston: Little, Brown, 1961. An anthology of twelve important Western plays by Sophocles, Shakespeare, Ibsen, Chekhov, Yeats, and others. The editor provides a valuable commentary after each play.

Michael Shurgot, "A Game of Cards in Steinbeck's *Of Mice and Men,*" *Steinbeck Quarterly,* vol. 15, nos. 1–2, Winter/Spring 1982. This essay focuses on the seemingly irrelevant games of solitaire played by George, showing how their carefully arranged placement underscores the elements of isolation, chance, and futility in the story.

John Steinbeck, introduction to *Short Novels of John Steinbeck*. New York: Viking, 1953. In an introduction to a collection that includes *The Red Pony, Tortilla Flat, Of Mice and Men, The Moon Is Down, Cannery Row*, and *The Wayward Bus*, Steinbeck provides a brief commentary on how each book came to be written.

E.W. Tedlock Jr. and C.V. Wicker, eds., *Steinbeck and His Critics: A Record of Twenty-Five Years*. Albuquerque: University of New Mexico Press, 1957. Includes critical essays on Steinbeck's work by seventeen noted critics as well as by the author himself.

Mark Van Doren, "*Of Mice and Men* by John Steinbeck," *Nation*, March 6, 1937. The literary editor for the *Nation* at the time *Of Mice and Men* was published, Van Doren offers harsh contemporary criticism of Steinbeck's plot and characterization.

Edmund Wilson, *The Boys in the Back Room: Notes on California Novelists*. San Francisco: Colt, 1941. A critical analysis of a number of California authors.

## Historical Background

William Dudley, ed., *The Great Depression: Opposing Viewpoints*. San Diego: Greenhaven, 1994. An anthology of essays that address various issues surrounding the Great Depression.

William S. Myers and Walter H. Newton, *The Hoover Administration: A Documented Narrative*. New York: Charles Scribner's Sons, 1936. A diary-like synopsis of Herbert Hoover's years in the White House, featuring extracts from the president's speeches and announcements.

Studs Terkel, *Hard Times: An Oral History of the Depression*. New York: Random House, 1970. The recollections of more than 160 Americans who lived through the Great Depression, collected by the noted journalist and author.

# Index

# Picture Credits

# About the Author

Bradley Steffens is a widely published poet, playwright, and essayist and the author of nineteen nonfiction books for young adults. He lives in Escondido, California, with his wife, Angela.